AREA OF OUTSTANDIN

JOURNEYS THROUGH
BRIGANTIA

TOP OF QUARLTON

VOLUME ELEVEN:

Circular Walks in
The East Lancashire Pennines

JOHN DIXON   JAANA JÄRVINEN

AUSSTEIGER FIELD GUIDE

JOURNEYS THROUGH BRIGANTIA

VOLUME ELEVEN:

CIRCULAR WALKS IN
THE EAST LANCASHIRE PENNINES

By

John Dixon & Jaana Järvinen

Copyright ⊕ John Dixon 2003
ALL RIGHTS RESERVED

Published by:
AUSSTEIGER PUBLICATIONS

Distributed by:
LANCASHIRE BOOKS
213 Chorley Old Road, Whittle-le-Woods, Chorley PR6 7NP
Tel. 01257-278613

Typeset & Printed by:
HARGREAVES STEEL LIMITED,
133 Henry Street, Church, Accrington, Lancashire BB5 4EP
Tel: 01254-230773

First edition 2003

ISBN 1 872764 07 X

The sketch maps in this book are intended to indicate the route in a general way.
Walkers should use Ordnance Survey Pathfinder maps to locate exact routes.

Whilst all the walks use established and definitive footpaths (unless otherwise stated
in the text), walkers are requested to respect the privacy of residents and not to stray
from the footpaths.

If you find that a footpath has been obstructed, please report the matter on your return
to: Nick Bamber, Area Network Officer, Guild House, Cross Street, Preston PR1 8RD
Tel: 01772 264681. Fax: 01772 263732.

PLEASE OBSERVE THE COUNTRY CODE.

Dedicated to the memory of Mrs Alice Smith, of Copster Green, and Mr Norman
Rawlings, of Salesbury — both now walking in higher places . . .

AUSSTEIGER PUBLICATIONS

Contents

INTRODUCTION..5

WALK 1: THROUGH ANCIENT HUNTING GROUNDS............................7
Ribchester, Stydd, Dutton, Greengore & Hurst Green
7 miles, 4 hours

WALK 2: OLD HALLS & DEER PARKS...19
Copster Green, Showley, Oxendale, Osbaldeston & Salesbury
6½ miles, 3½ hours

WALK 3: BY WAY OF CUTHBERT'S RESTING STOP............................33
Mellor, Ramsgreave & Clayton-le-Dale
4½ miles, 3 hours

WALK 4: LAST MARTYR TO CROMWELL...43
Witton, Pleasington, Samlesbury & Billinge
8 miles, 4 hours

WALKS 5 & 6: HOGHTON BOTTOMS & THE YELLOW HILLS.......................59
Witton Park, Pleasington, Hoghton, Riley Green & Cherry Tree
8 miles & 5 miles

WALK 7: THE ANCIENTS LOOK DOWN...73
Brinscall, Round Loaf, Pikestones & White Coppice
9 miles & 5miles, 6 hours & 3 hours respectively

WALK 8: THE STONES OF ICE & MEN...85
Turton Heights & Dimple
12 miles, 6 hours

WALK 9: LIVESEY-CUM-TOCKHOLES...93
Darwen, Livesey & Tockholes
9 miles, 5 hours

WALK 10: MOORLAND TOWER & WOODLAND HALL.......................107
Tockholes, Roddlesworth & Darwen Moor
8 miles, 4 hours

WALK 11: A TRAMP AROUND TURTON...115
Turton Tower, Affetside, Quarlton & Chapeltown
8 miles, 5 hours

WALK 12: CRUCKS & CASTLES...123
Rivington & Winter Hill
11 miles, 6 hours or Shorter Walks: 6 & 4½ miles

AUSSTEIGER HISTORICAL FIELD GUIDES

Historic Walks around the Pendle Way   1990

Bowland-Pendle Challenge Trail   1993

JOURNEYS THROUGH BRIGANTIA

VOLUME ONE: 1990
Craven, Airedale & Wharfedale

VOLUME TWO: 1990
Ribblesdale, Malham & Central Wharfedale

VOLUME THREE:
Lower Wharfedale, Washburndale & Ilkley Moor

VOLUME FOUR: 1991
'Beyond the Hill of Winds': Upper Ribblesdale,
The Three Peaks & Upper Wharfedale

VOLUME FIVE:
Nidderdale, Knaresborough & Wensleydale

VOLUME SIX:
Swaledale, Teesdale & the Vale of Eden

VOLUME SEVEN:
The Lune Valley & The Howgill Fells

VOLUME EIGHT: 1992 & 1993
The Forest of Bowland

VOLUME NINE: 1993
The Ribble Valley

VOLUME TEN:
Pendle & The Bronte South Pennines

VOLUME ELEVEN: 1994
The East Lancashire Pennines

Distributors: Lancashire Books, 213 Chorley Old Road,
                 Whittle-le-Woods, Chorley PR6 7NP. Tel. 01257-278613

INTRODUCTION

In this volume of 'Historic Walks' I go back to an area that has been known to me since boyhood, and returning some thirty-odd years later I find that very little of the rural splendour and tranquility of the region that I remembered has changed. The same families farm the valley pastures and uplands, though with less labour and more subsidy than in former times. Some of the villages have expanded as urban incomers seek retreat from their town and city workplace, but not in such a way as to become merely sprawling extensions of the former industrial centres of Bolton, Preston and Blackburn.

The northern section of this work takes in those prospects around the lower Darwen and Ribble river valleys encompassing all those rustic hamlets and hidden nooks that are to be found by the discerning wanderer between Hurst Green and Riley Green — a superb district for family rambles and lone explorations.

The West Pennine Moors are those high open spaces of moorland, valleys and reservoirs which rise above the mill towns of Darwen, Bolton and Greater Manchester. The high moors can seem bleak and forbidding on an overcast day, but on a clear day they attract one like a magnet, to wander the moors seemingly for ever. The moors are marked by man's settlement and activity by features which go back many thousands of years. Traces of early man's endeavours can be seen throughout the area. Their tombs, homesteads and stone monuments point to the existence of a stable and settled community in those times.

Today's harsh climate and poor soils support sparse grasses, on which sheep and some cattle graze. Many of the old sheep farms are long gone, remembered only by the low walls of their ruins. These farmers often supported their families by having other jobs. Small quarries provided stone for walls, buildings and millstones, the rough gritty rock being good for grinding corn. The hill-folk also spun, wove and bleached wool, from which skills and ideas grew, eventually feeding and supporting the Industrial Revolution. As our towns grew, their way of life changed drastically, part of their lands giving way to the vast new reservoirs needed to provide the lifeblood and energy reserves for new enterprise. Years later, the sons and daughters of those early mill-folk have once again returned to the hills and moors, not to farm and toil with stone, but to relax and freely stroll in the good clean air. For a small time the pace of modern life is forgotten as the near landscape draws us in.

The walks described here are more rambles of exploration and are designed to give the native and visitor alike a greater awareness of man's role in the development of these uplands. Let the moorland walk be a time for reflection, to learn to know where you are now and where you came from. Enjoy the hills which have for so long been so closely a part of the lives, economies and culture of the people of the East Lancashire Pennines.   — John Dixon, Clitheroe, 2003

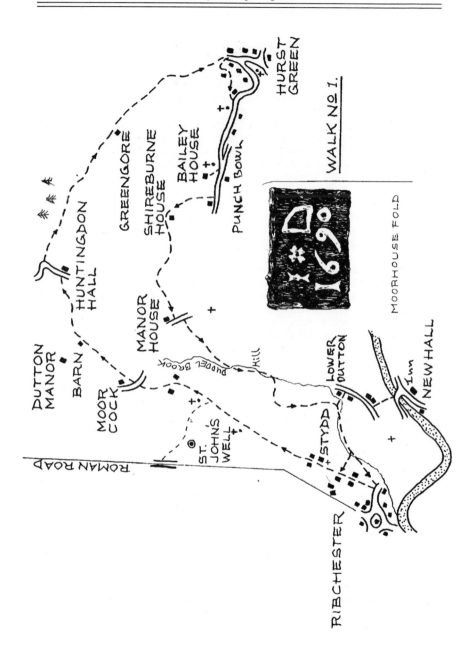

WALK 1
THROUGH ANCIENT HUNTING GROUNDS

Ribchester, Stydd, Dutton,
Greengore & Hurst Green

7 miles, 4 hours,

MAP: *O.S. sheet SD 63/73 PATHFINDER*

LUNCH: *Bailey Arms, Hurst Green*

START: *Ribchester Car Park or Hurst Green*

This walk takes us up through Dutton into the old deer park of Stonyhurst and on down to lunch at Hurst Green. After visiting the haunt of a local highwayman we make our way over the fields to return down Duddel Brook — a site of pre-industrial enterprise — to the Ribchester district. A rewarding walk in all its aspects.

Ribchester to Stydd Chapel
Walk down the Blackburn road to go left up Stydd lane at Stonebridge. Walk on past the Shireburn Almshouses to the Chapel of St. Saviour.

Stydd Chapel
The earliest reference to the chapel and ancient hospital at Stydd is in the Quo Warranto proceedings of 1292 when it was proved that the Knights Hospitalers had acquired the estate around 1265 from Adam de Blackburn, chaplain-warden of the house of St. Saviour at Dutton under Longridge.

An undated charter (approximately 1150) informs us that Alan de Singleton confirmed land to the chapel and hospital. So Stydd had a very early foundation indeed. This is reflected by the Norman doorway and windows in the north wall.

The majority of the chapel is Early English from the time of the Hospitalers; the rest, including the font, belongs to the early 16th century.

In those early times the building we see today would have served as chapel/hospital combined, serving the needs of a very small community. Other buildings would have existed — dwellings for the brethren and a farm.

The inside of the church is very austere, but nevertheless a few gems are to be found. The late Perpendicular font is of dark gritstone, octagonal in shape, each side with a shield bearing sacred, heraldic and other devices. This was a gift from Sir Thomas Pemberton, preceptor of Newland, under which Stydd was a camera (estate). The screen and pulpit are of very simple character, built of oak in the 17th century.

On the floor of the sanctuary are several grave slabs, the most interesting being that of Sir Adam and Lady Alicia de Cliderow of Salesbury Hall. The slab is damaged but the floreated design of a knight and his lady can be made out. The Cliderows were buried here around 1350.

Outside, in the old graveyard, stands an ancient cross base, thought to have come from Duddel Hill above Stydd.

St. John's Well, Dutton

This ancient spring, that has never been known to run dry, bubbles out of the ground by the side of Stydd Brook. Its waters have remarkable healing properties and were once used by the Knights Hospitaler to cure eye and joint ailments.

I have tried these waters and find them pleasant and efficacious. This well was first pointed out to me by Mr William Byrne of Ribchester, to whom go my many thanks.

Stydd Church to Moor Cock Inn

Walk on through the farmyard, through gate and over the stile by the red gate. Follow the well-worn track up the field to the right-hand corner gate. Over the stile and follow left-hand hedge to a footbridge (the remains of an ancient cross are in the corner of the field on your left). Cross the footbridge and walk straight across the field to go over a stile. Walk up the field on a slight right diagonal to pass through a field gate. Follow track up to Duddel Hill Farm and on to the main road. The Moor Cock Inn is the first house on the right, up the road.

Moor Cock Farm

Up until 1923 when it lost its licence, this farm was known as the Moor Cock Inn. Above the front door is a most colourful datestone of 1775 with the initials B.B. — those of Benjamin Bulcock.

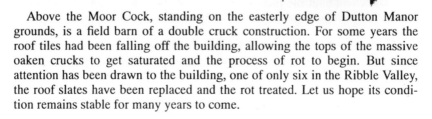

Above the Moor Cock, standing on the easterly edge of Dutton Manor grounds, is a field barn of a double cruck construction. For some years the roof tiles had been falling off the building, allowing the tops of the massive oaken crucks to get saturated and the process of rot to begin. But since attention has been drawn to the building, one of only six in the Ribble Valley, the roof slates have been replaced and the rot treated. Let us hope its condition remains stable for many years to come.

Moor Cock Inn to Huntingdon Hall

Walk back to Duddel Hill Farm entrance on the bend of the road. Cross the hedge stile opposite. Walk on and over stile in the fence by the tree line. Walk on up the field on a right diagonal to pass through a kissing-gate in the far right hand corner. Left, over the bridge and after 20 yards turn right and follow the path up through the wood and over the stile. Walk up to the left, past the barn to go over stile by gate.

Follow right hand fence to pass over stile. Follow the brook up to the copse. Walk right, around the copse and through the field gate. Follow the path around the brow of the hill, and on through wooden gates to Huntingdon Hall.

HUNTINGDON HALL

Huntingdon Hall

The Hall and lands in this part of Dutton are named after one Robert of Huntingdon, who came here from the Abbey of Selby in 1277. After the death of his son, Roger, a feud ensued between Robert and Beatrix, widow of Roger, over the ownership of his son's land.

During the 16th century, Richard Crombleholme acquired lands in Dutton and Bailey and built the present Huntingdon Hall some time after in 1619. His initials with this date are carved upon the front door-head.

The Hall is H-shaped with a facade of mullioned windows of six lights below, five above, and three in the gables. Above the entrance gateway is the weight of an old cheese press mounted upon a pillar; also some Roman fragments are built into the walls of the grounds, one piece of which is the same as those built into Connerie Bridge near the De Tabley Arms.

Huntingdon Hall to Greengore

Walk up the road to go over a stile by gate. Right, and follow right hand fence on, over stile, on and over next stile. From here you get a good view of Pendle with Stonyhurst College in the foreground. Walk directly on to go down to old trackway by wall. Right, and follow trackway down to Greengore.

GREENGORE

Greengore

Standing on the side of an old moorland trackway is the imposingly strange house of Greengore. Mention of the house was first recorded in 1314 when 'Thomas de Greengore confirmed to Adam his son, certain land in Bailey, excepting the Greengore'.

During the 16th and 17th centuries the house was used as a hunting lodge for the Stonyhurst Deer Park and is said to have played host to the Lancastrian Kings.

Greengore to Hurst Green

Continue on down the farm lane, left at the junction and on to cross Dean Brook Bridge. Follow track on to the Almshouses and on down the road to the Bailey Arms.

Old Crosses around Hurst Green

The old village cross is situated in a garden on the west side of the Green. The short trefoil head and shaft are set in a flight of three steps known as a calvary.

The Warren Cross

The Warren Cross takes the form of a simple incised cross cut into a large stone built into a wall on the lane past Warren Farm (SD 686381).

Local legend holds that the stone was brought from Cutler Bailey's house in Dean Bottom over a hundred years ago. Cutler was murdered by his wife many years before this by her putting poison into his tea and to escape detection broke the teapot against the wall of the house.

It is said that the reason why the poison was put into the teapot and not into a drinking-cup was that when her husband arrived home he would drink the tea straight out of the teapot spout. By putting strychnine into the teapot, his wife found a most effective and permanent way of curing him of his habit.

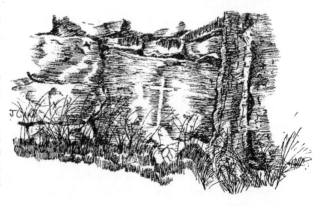

She was later tried and hanged at Lancaster.

The incised cross is said to mark the stone on which the teapot broke.

Shire Lane Cross

Where Shire Lane joins the old high-way that comes down from Greengore stands the pedestal of the Shire Lane Cross.

Gorton Rake Cross (SD 676379)

The section of Shire Lane which runs of rising ground is known as Gorton Rake.

In the field behind the roadside seat, almost hidden beneath a holly and haw-thorn hedge, is a cross pedestal which is all that remains of the Gorton Rake Cross.

Cross Gills Cross

This cross stands in a prominent posi-tion on the top of Chitterick Hill by Cross Gills Farm (originally the farm was also known as Chitterick, Cross Gills is a corruption of the name of a former tenant, a Mr Croskell).

Only the base is ancient, the cross and pedestal were erected by the Rector of Stonyhurst in 1883 and blessed by Bishop Penswick.

CROSS GILLS,

HURST GREEN

Hurst Green to the Punch Bowl Inn

Walk up to the Shireburn Almshouse and turn down the lane opposite Smithy Row and at the end of the high hedge turn left and walk on to meet with a driveway. Pass through the white gate on the right and walk on past the converted mill to cross footbridge by side of house.

Walk up, noticing the lovely gardens and waterfall down on the right, to enter field via stile. Walk up the field to pass over stile and on to pass through farmyard onto Shire Lane. Follow lane to the right to the main road and the Punch Bowl Inn. Bailey House is on the right.

THE PUNCH BOWL

Punch Bowl Inn

The Punch Bowl Inn stands on the Longridge to Clitheroe road opposite Bailey House. The frontage is always well maintained, reflecting its two hundred years' standing. A datestone above the front doorway informs us that the inn was built in 1793 for a family with the initials R.C.E. Inside is a fine restaurant catering for those who only wish a bar snack right through to the evening dinner.

The pub's two inn signs recall the tale of the capture of the highwayman, Ned King, by officers of the Crown. Ned is reputed to have taken refuge at the inn. After a series of events he was captured, hanged and later gibboted on the gallows at Three Turns, Gallows Lane.

His ghost haunted the musicians' gallery in the dining room for many years until it was exorcised in 1942 by a priest from Stonyhurst College.

Bailey House

Bailey House is a late 17th century farmhouse that is now a single dwelling house, converted from its original two halves. The frontage displays many fine mullioned windows with slender hood moulding above the ground floor and gable windows. The west gable is a very good example of watershot stonework.

To the west of Bailey House stands Shireburn House. Although built in 1675, little can be made out from that former age, except the old mullioned window.

Punch Bowl Inn to Manor House

Walk on up the road to go first right up to Shireburn House. Pass through wooden gate on the right of Shireburn House driveway and follow old track, over stream, to go over stile by field gate. Follow left hand fence to go over stile. Cross the field on a slight right diagonal to corner of wood to pass over stile into field. Walk on passing corner of far hedge and on, keeping left, to go over footbridge. Follow right hand fence, through gateway to enter Manor House farmyard by gate. Walk on to the roadway.

Manor House and Duddel Brook Mill

The old Manor House, although a listed building, is sadly falling into ruin. The first floor has fallen in and it is not advised to make a close inspection. A few mullioned windows peer out through the ivy and undergrowth and a Tudor style doorhead can be seen. In the grounds stands an old 17th century cheese press, moss-covered, having seen its last days. (* March 1993 — the house has now been restored to a good standard).

The walk down to Lower Dutton passes the ruin of Dutton Mill. In its heyday combs were manufactured by the local inhabitants. Dutton Brook provided the power and careful inspection of the site will reveal the wheel house, mill lodge and race and the fine stone weir providing the head of water.

Manor House to Lower Dutton

Turn left and walk down the road a short way to pass over stile by gate on right. Cross the field to pass over corner stile on left at wood. Follow the edge of the wood down to enter wood via stile. Follow path to the left and on down to cross the stream. Continue on and up to meet with higher path below stile. Take the left hand path that leads us down to the site of the old mill via two footbridges. Continue on downstream to pass over footbridge. Walk up to enter field via stile. Walk on to pass over stile by gate on left. Walk down the field to pass over stile by gate and on down to pass over bridge*. Walk to the left to pass over fence-stile. Left, and over next stile. Walk up to meet with road by hedge-stile to the left of the gate. Walk down to Lower Dutton.

LOWER DUTTON
COTTAGES

Lower Dutton Cottages

This group of delightful 17th century cottages stand below Dutton Hall on Gallows Lane, so called after the gibbot that stood further up the lane at Three Turns. The local highwayman, Ned King, was displayed upon the gibbot having been tried and hanged for his crimes. Before his capture, the unfortunate rogue is said to have sought refuge in the Punch Bowl Inn.

* This way takes us down to Ribchester Bridge but if you wish to return to Stydd then use the following directions from bridge above.

Walk over to the right to pass over stile by gate and on to go over next stile. The path now leads us on to go over a footbridge and then a stile and over to the right to pass over further stile. Walk up to the left to the Almshouses.

Lower Dutton to Ribchester Bridge

Walk down the road to go left over stile after farm. Walk across the field to go over stile onto riverbank. Walk on to Ribchester Bridge.

New Hall, Clayton-le-Dale

Standing proud on the bank of the Ribble near Ribchester Bridge is the newly restored Jacobean house of New Hall.

The house was built by George Talbot in 1665. George, a Royalist during the Civil Wars, was captured at Preston in 1643. He returned to Salesbury Hall, a timber-framed house not unlike Samlesbury Hall, when peace was restored, to start work on his 'new' stone-built house at Clayton-le-Dale.

George was from that family of Talbots, Lords of Salesbury and Bashall, who rode forth in 1464 to effect the capture of King Henry VI, who was seeking refuge at Waddington Hall. They captured the King at Brungerley hipping stones whilst he was attempting to escape. He was thence carried bound to a horse to London and imprisoned in the Tower.

Even today some see the Talbots' action as an act of treachery, but given those troubled times who is to say what was right or wrong.

Above the first floor porch window is a moulded panel, on which is depicted a talbot — a breed of hound — the crest of the Talbots. It was this

hound that gave Sir Arthur Conan Doyle, when a student at Stonyhurst College, the idea for his book "The Hound of the Baskervilles".

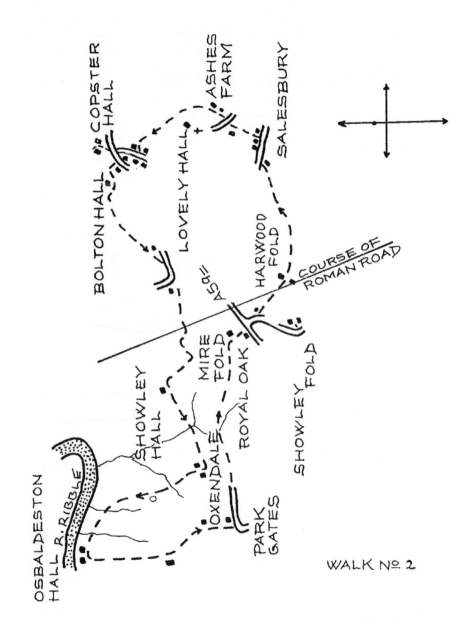

WALK No 2

Walk 2

OLD HALLS AND DEER PARKS

Copster Green, Showley, Oxendale,
Osbaldeston & Salesbury
6½ miles, 3½ hours

MAP: *O.S. sheet SD 63/73 PATHFINDER*

LUNCH: *Royal Oak, Clayton-le-Dale*

START: *Copster Green*

Today we set out from Copster Green and cross several wooded ravines, that hide away many an ancient pile, on our way down to the former Osbaldeston ferry crossing of the Ribble. We return by way of Showley Vale to visit Lovely Hall before ending our ramble on those cottage-lined greens at Copster.

Copster Green

In the days before the advent of motor car ownership, Copster Green was a popular picnic spot for Blackburnians en route from the Wilpshire tram stop to Ribchester bridge.

The greens still afford a pleasant stopping point on a fine summer's day, with its many cottages possessing neat garden frontages which in season are clothed with a profusion of rich plants and flowers.

Copster Green village is laid out around a series of old filled-in and grassed-over quarries, giving the place a rugged beauty — only a busy main road spoils its picturesque setting. The deer park is recalled in the name of the local inn. The Park Gate Inn restaurant is popular with visitors to the area.

Copster Green Cross (SD 677342)

This small monument has recently been re-erected by the owner in the front garden. I am informed that it has stood near to this spot since well before the First World War.

Could it be the lost Lovely Hall Cross? I can only compare the round top stone to the Toches Stone in St. Stephen's churchyard, Tockholes. The strangely tooled shaft suggests that it could be Roman, perhaps a small altar for votive offerings?

The Copster Green Angel Stone

This curious figure is set above the doorway of a cottage that stands on the old road that ran east from the village. Could this fragment be all that remains of the old Dinckley Chapel, recorded in a c.1610 report on the clergy as being a 'chapel but no reader' and belonging to Dinckley Hall?

This chapel, now lost, is thought to have stood in the south-west corner of the parish, near the Salesbury boundary stone below Wheatley Farm. The field name here is 'Chapel Field' which is far too small to be of agricultural use and thus could well be the site of this chapel.

Copster Green to Copster Hall

Walk down the green to the road opposite Park Gate Inn. Turn right, walking down the roadway to go first left up to Copster Hall.

Copster Hall

Sited on top of an outcrop of rock above Copster Green stands Copster Hall. The house has a datestone of 1615 above the front door, but the present building has been totally rebuilt since that time. It was then known as Copthurst Hall, home of the Parker family who held lands here until the 18th century.

In their day the hall was used as a hunting lodge for the great deer park of

Salesbury Hall. It is hard to imagine now that the surrounding lands were once heavily wooded and populated by red deer and other game animals.

The east-facing front of the house displays two fine early 17th century mullioned and transomed windows on its upper floor, re-used from the earlier building.

The original level of the Jacobean building can be determined by the position of the small mullioned windows which are near to the ground on the north wall. Apparently a large part of the earlier house had been demolished down to a level of about six foot and the rubble levelled out giving a higher ground level. An inspection of what are now the cellars confirmed this. The earlier level can be seen again if one examines the southerly section of the building, which now serves as a barn.

COPSTER HALL

On the outside of the south wall a hood moulding and label show the position of a large, first floor, mullioned and transomed window. Inside the barn, on the west wall, can be seen the top of an enormous inglenook fireplace, its lower portion buried beneath the floor.

An upper floor fireplace can be seen above this in the hay loft. This discovery explains the large rectangular projection at the south of the west wall — a chimney stack of great proportions. What a grand house this must have been!

Copster Hall to Bolton Hall

Walk back to the Park Gate Inn to turn right down the lane by the side of the inn, then fork left down to Bolton Hall.

BOLTON HALL

Bolton Hall

Hidden away down an old farm lane stands Bolton Hall. Set in a low and sheltered situation on the left bank of Park Brook this is a true relic of Cromwellian days. The Hall was built by the Bolton family in 1655 and little has changed since that time.

It is a two-storey house with low mullioned windows and a stone-slated overhanging roof. All the windows have hood mouldings above and diamond-shaped leaded lights. Over the four-centred arch is a date, 1655, with the initials L.B.M.

The Bolton family have lived in these parts since the 13th century when, in about 1270, one Richard de Bolton (Bolton-by-Bowland) married Agnes, daughter of Ranulf de Salesbury. The barn adjoining the hall is also of the period and displays some splendid timberwork on the inside.

The present owner deserves full credit for the restoration work carried out on the building. If others do only half as well, what a great contribution it would be to the heritage of the North West.

Bolton Hall to Showley Hall

Continue on up and along the lane to pass over stile by gate at its end (do not pass over stile on right). Continue directly on along edge of field to pass over stile on left and on to pass over next stile. Cross the field directly to pass over stile by gate. Follow fenced-off trackway to road via stile in gate. Right, and walk along the road to go down the lane at corner by boulder-marked drive. The lane leads us down to Showley Hall.

Showley Hall

Showley Hall stands on a high situation between two small ravines on the south side of the River Ribble. The house was originally built around three sides of a quadrangle. Sadly, all but the central block at the south end had been demolished before 1887 and even this portion has been largely rebuilt.

The doorway is flanked by Ionic columns with a richly moulded classical lintel above; upon one of the capitals is a strange looking creature peering out from the stonework. Only one window preserves its ancient stone mullions, the rest being of a 19th century design.

A private chapel once stood to the north of the house and was used by Catholics living within the area. The furnishing and architectural pieces were moved by the Walmesley family to their seat at Dunkenhalgh in Clayton-le-Moors. Sited in front of the house are the mediaeval fish ponds; though much silted-up, they remain complete.

During the 14th century, Showley hall was the home of the de Blackburn family. John de Blackburn of Showley was one of the twenty-one barons known as Lords Ordainers who ruled the country during part of the reign of Edward II.

Edward, during the first few years of his reign, ruled with his epicene friend and favourite, Piers Gaveston. Together, they ruled badly. The Barons, rightly disgusted with such behaviour, took over rule and sent Gaveston into exile.

Gaveston did not go away at once, however, and a number of Barons, John de Blackburn included, caught and beheaded him. Edward did not forgo his then unnatural acts and later suffered a most terrible fate at the hands of the Barons, far too horrific to record here.

Showley was later the home of the Walmesley family. One, William Walmesley of Showley, was tried at Liverpool Castle in 1716 on a charge of complicity in the Jacobite Rebellion of 1715 but was acquitted.

Another noted resident was Francis Petre, Roman Catholic Bishop of Amoria (the Northern District). Bishop Petre resided here for many years until his death in 1775. His tomb can be seen in the church of St. Saviour, Stydd.

Showley Hall to Oxendale Hall

Pass through the farmyard with the barn on your right and walk down the field to pass over stile by gate. Cross the field heading towards the bottom left hand corner where you will find a stile. Over, then down to cross the footbridge. Walk up through the wood to pass over stile. Follow fence on to Oxendale Hall.

Oxendale Hall

OXENDALE

Such is the restoration work done to this building that, standing at its front, it would come as no surprise if a troop of Roundheads were to march down the driveway. Our thanks go out to its owner.

Oxendale Hall stands on a high ground to the south of the Ribble and is well sheltered by woods on the north side. It is a picturesque, three-storey stone built house with many fine mullioned windows. The front has been well

restored and all the windows are new with the exception of those of the top floor in the gables and over the porch. At the rear the original 17th century windows remain. The door has a four-centred arch and the initials of Lawrence and Rosamund Osbaldeston and the date 1658. A lead rainwater spout-head on the side of the porch has the initials of William Fox of Goosnargh, yeoman, who purchased Oxendale in 1714.

The barn at Oxendale is one of the few cruck-built type to survive in the area.

A Roman Catholic mission was established here around 1834 and, on October 25th 1838, the chapel of St. Mary was opened on the border of the township with Mellor.

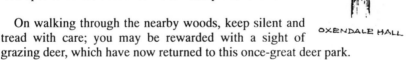

On walking through the nearby woods, keep silent and tread with care; you may be rewarded with a sight of grazing deer, which have now returned to this once-great deer park.

Oxendale Hall to Osbaldeston Hall

Walk past the barn to enter field via gate. Cross the field, heading slightly to the left to pass over stile above wooded ravine. Walk directly down to cross stream and walk up to pass over fence stile. Cross the field keeping the tree-lined pond on your left, to go over stile in bottom left-hand corner. Walk down to cross the brook and walk up through the wood to pass over stile. Walk on to pass through gate and follow track down to go over stile on right. Walk on past the front of Osbaldeston Hall to farm lane.

OSBALDESTON HALL

Osbaldeston Hall

Osbaldeston Hall stands majestic on the bank of the River Ribble and was once set within a deer park. The house is mainly late-Elizabethan with some Tudor work inside.

OSBALDESTON HALL

On the doorhead to the rear of the building are carved the arms of Osbaldeston impaling Bradley, with the date 1593, and the initials of John Osbaldeston and Ellen (Bradley), his wife, and on either side the initials T.O. and T.D., the former perhaps those of Thomas, their son. The stone evidently belonged to the older part of the house and has been used in later building.

Height, 2 feet 6 inches.

The house was originally moated and small remains can still be made out. The west end of the house was once the gallery. Tradition holds that there was a chapel projecting from the north wall, near the kitchen door.

Set in the wall at this point was once a rude figure, said to represent Hercules and to be from the Roman Fort at Ribchester. The figure was removed to the Old Hall, Tabley.

The family of Osbaldeston, one of the most noted in Lancashire, took their surname from the district which means 'the tun of Oswald'. In 1390, John, son of Geoffrey de Osbaldeston, was in Ireland in the

King's service and in the retinue of Sir John Stanley. He was knighted at St. Maxence by Henry V on 13th October 1415 before the Battle of Agincourt.

In the spring of 1417, he went to France, again in the retinue of the King, and with other Lancashire knights before Louviers and Rouen in the summer of 1418, and at Gisors the following year. By marriage, he became Lord of Chadlington Manor, Oxon, and ancestor of the Osbaldestons of those parts.

Alexander Osbaldeston fought at Flodden Field under the Earl of Derby and was later knighted. He was sheriff of the county 1527/8 and died 17th January 1544.

Edward Osbaldeston, a priest educated at Rheims in 1585, was sent on the English Mission of 1589. After 'working' the North for some years, he was betrayed and suffered death at York on 16th November 1594 at the age of 34.

Edward Osbaldeston, a great scholar and sportsman, was born in 1573 and was knighted at Lathom House by James I in 1617; he died in 1637. Alexander, his son, had his estates sequestered for recusancy, though he had never been in arms against the Parliament. In 1650, in response to his petition, an order was made to allow him one third of his estates. Alexander, grandson of the above, was the last Osbaldeston of the Lancashire line; he died in 1752.

Osbaldeston Hall to Mire Fold

Follow the lane up passing New House and the Horse Riding School to Park Gate (dated inside porch 1675). Turn left and follow the tree-lined lane down past the grounds of Oxendale Hall to enter wooded ravine by two old gate posts. Walk down the path to go over footbridge. Follow path up to go over stile. Walk on up to the field. Cross the field centrally, keeping the hollow on your left, over to Mire Fold farm gate and stile. Enter Mire Fold.

Park Gate, Osbaldeston

This creeper-clad cottage stands at the head of the old deer park of the Osbaldestons. Though the house has changed in style since its foundation, it still retains its early datestone. Set above the doorway the stone reads: JAMES SHORAC 1675 (James Shorrock).

PARK GATE

Mire Fold

MIRE FOLD

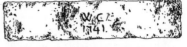

The farm at Mire Fold is noted for its stained glass window. This depicts three hooded children warming their hands over a fire.

The window is one of a pair and originally came from Woodfold Hall, which is now in ruin. On the barn, clumsy initials and a date are carved: W.C. 1741.

Mire Fold to Harwood Fold

ROYAL OAK

Go through the farmyard, on up to Longsight Road at The Royal Oak. Cross into Showley Road. Walk up the road to go left down the trackway at the 'Kennels' sign. Walk on to Harwood Fold.

HARWOOD FOLD.

HARWOOD FOLD

Harwood Fold

I was always of the opinion that Harwood Fold was demolished in the 19th century when the farmhouse that stands today was built. But on inspecting the barn and farmbuildings I observed, built into the present fabric, the remains of two cottages along with a much-worn date tablet. The tablet is set into the barn wall that stands between the two old cottages.

The Fold takes its name from a yeoman family of that name, one of whom, John Harwood, was a governor of Blackburn Grammar School in 1681. His son William restored the farmhouse, as is recorded by his initials W.H.E. and the date 1728 upon the stone tablet built into the barn (the stone is now much-worn and a new farmhouse replaces the earlier one).

SHOWLEY FOLD

Showley Fold

Showley Fold is a group of 17th and 18th century buildings, the oldest being an ivy-covered farmhouse at the bottom of the lane. This house has a central porch and low mullioned windows.

SHOWLEY FOLD

Carved in the door lintel are the initials J.D.T. and the date 1747. The house is older in parts than that date and formerly belonged to the Cowper family. The stone in the angle of the porch gable is dated 1828, with the initials of Thomas Ainsworth, the builder of Showley Fold as it appears today.

The rear section of the roof warrants inspection, the Dutch-gable arrangement being uncommon for the period. The house near the roadway gives the appearance of once being a toll-house, but I know this is not the case.

Harwood Fold to Ashes Farm

*Follow the trackway through the Fold to where it turns down to the Kennels.
Here, in front of you, are a gate and stile. Cross over the stile and follow the
path to the right of the pylon to Clayton Hey Fold. Pass through the kissing-
gate and walk on up to the road. Turn right and walk up the road.*

*After passing the first four houses on the left, leave the road by the stile on
your left. Follow the left hand fence down to go over a garden stile onto the
house driveway. Walk up the driveway onto the road. Turn right and walk up
the road to go left down Ashes Farm trackway. Walk on, passing the cottage
to the farmyard.*

Ashes Farm

By the lane leading to the farm stands the
weight of an old cheese press and in the nearby
Ashes Cottage garden is a curious acorn-shaped
stone, possibly a decorative finial off some
grand building.

At Ashes Farm itself can be found a datestone of 1673 built into a wall by the side of
the farmhouse door. The stone came from Ben
Fold, an old farmstead in the area which is now demolished.

Lovely Hall

Set within gardens of the first water is the ancient palatial residence of Lovely
Hall. For five centuries, this estate was held by the families of Bolton and
Parker.

In 1246, Robert de Bolton had lands in Salesbury and
Clayton. A John Bolton was the last in line of this family
and passed his estates to trustees in 1508, for the settlement
upon his daughter Elizabeth and her then husband John, son
of John Singleton of Chingle Hall. Elizabeth later married
Hugh Parker and then James Halsall. Richard Parker, son of
Elizabeth and Hugh, succeeded to the estate around 1592.

LOVELY HALL

After the Civil Wars, John Parker of Lovely Hall had his
estates sold by the Treason Trustees in 1654 for his delin-
quency. In 1711, another John Parker sold Lovely Hall to

Edmund Winder of Clayton-le-Dale. Edmund's son, John, held the estate in 1735, as appears from his initials and the date upon the easing pipes on the front of the house. In 1757, his son Edmund sold the estate to Piers Starkie of Huntroyd, whose descendants manage the estate to this day.

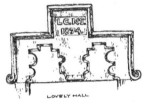

The hall is a two-storey stone built house with stone tiled roofs, erected in the early 17th century, but very much altered in 1735 and again in the later 19th century. The fireplace at the east end of the

hall is 10ft wide with a stone arch 6ft 6ins high, on which is carved the date 1712. On the front lawn stands a sundial with the date 1668, and the initials C.H. and R.S. — this originally came from Huntroyd.

Ashes Farm to Copster Green

Facing the entrance to Ashes Farm walk to the left and around to go over stile in hedgerow. Walk up to the low ruins. From here walk up to the left by a half-fallen hawthorn. Then follow the tree-line down the field to pass over a footbridge and stile over on the left. Walk up to the right to pass over stile and on up to the left to enter Copster Green by houses.

As Barons day turns into night,
Others rise to follow hounds.
But days are short for squirely Knights,
Now walkers tread their 'out of bounds'.

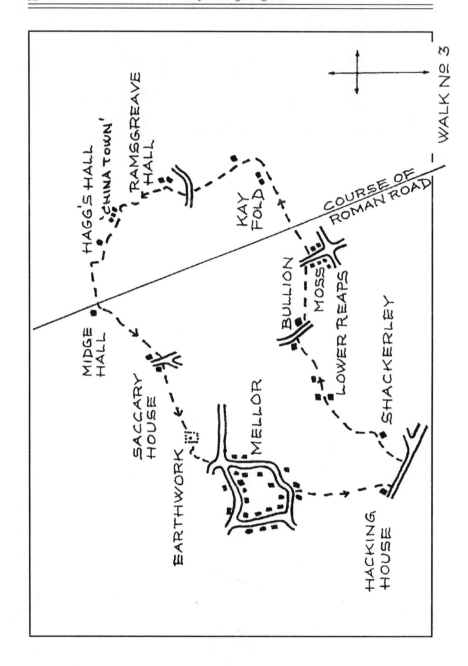

WALK № 3

Walk 3

BY WAY OF CUTHBERT'S RESTING STOP

Mellor, Ramsgreave, Clayton-le-Dale

4½ miles, 3 hours

MAP: *O.S. sheets SD 63/73 & 62/72 PATHFINDER*

START: *Mellor*

This walk leads us from the hill-top village of Mellor to follow the Blackburn Borough boundary to Ramsgreave. After a pleasing brookside ramble through Showley Vale we climb onto the moor above Mellor to explore ancient earthworks sited there. A pleasing walk with fine views over the Ribble Valley.

Mellor Village to Hacking House

From the top road by the Traders Arms, walk down Nickey Lane to enter Whitecroft Lane and walk on to go left at footpath sign by converted barn. Walk through the yard and garden to pass over stile into field. Walk down the grassed-over trackway opposite to pass through bottom gate. Walk on down the field to pass over footbridge by trees. Follow fence down to enter Hacking House farmyard via gates.

Hacking House

Hacking House is a very solid looking 17th century farmhouse. Above the front door is a door-head with the date 1697. The house retains its mullioned windows both to the front and rear, all very pleasing.

HACKING HOUSE

The road from Blackburn to Mellor Village was named Staingate; the land between it and the road to Showley was called 'Haukenchaw'; from the brook between Blackburn and Mellor called 'Hauekesshae' brook ran the ditch 'del Hackinbothe'.

HACKING HOUSE

This ditch runs westward from Long Row on Barker Lane through to Whinney Lane and, although it gives an indication of being an old trackway, this is doubtful for it runs along the hillside in an apparently predetermined line through Long Row to the site of a large covered well lying over the east side wall of Barker Lane. What purpose the ditch served is unknown.

Hacking House to Shackerley

Walk down the farm lane onto the roadway, turn left and walk on to turn left into Shackerley Farm gateway. Follow trackway on to the farmhouse.

Shackerley Farm

This 17th century farmstead gave its name to the Shackerley Toll Gate that used to stand on Preston New Road below the old Yew Tree Inn. Shackerley displays many of its ancient mullioned windows, though most have been altered over the ages.

The place-name 'Shackerley' is interesting; its derivation is 'Robbers Wood', perhaps a reference to the highwaymen of old.

One local story relates that on 21st January 1795, Mr Thomas Harwood of Mellor was returning home from Preston on horseback when he was stopped at Swill Brook by four footpads, one of whom held a pistol at him whilst another seized the reins of his bridle. He was overpowered by two of the men who held each of his arms whilst he was robbed of fifty pounds, with which the villains escaped.

SHACKERLEY FARM

Shackerley to Lower Reaps

Walk into the higher field. Walk directly up to the trees and follow hedgerow left to go over stile on the right. Follow left-hand fence, over stile and on over another stile by gate onto farm trackway. Turn right and walk down to Lower Reaps.

Lower Reaps

Lower Reaps is a most attractive 17th century farmstead. Only the west wing of the house displays its ancient mullioned windows with hood mouldings. The gardens to the front of the house, with the little stream wandering through it, make Lower Reaps very pleasing to the eye.

Lower Reaps to Ramsgreave Hall

*Walk past the front of the farmhouse, through farm gate and follow farm lane
to roadway. Turn right and walk down the road to turn left into farmyard.
Walk directly through farmyard and into field. Follow right-hand hedgerow
on to enter Barker Lane by stile near end cottage.*

*Cross the road to find path by side of modern house. Walk down, over stile,
to follow brookside pathway, through hedgerow, over fence stile (at this point
you are on a line with the Roman road, notice the paving stones from the road
near the brook) onto rugby field.*

*Follow stream on across Kay Fold farm track to pass through wall gate.
Follow stream on, then left-hand wall, to go over fence stile. Walk on
following left-hand fence to go left over stile by wall. Follow right-hand
fence/hedgerow/wall up over stiles and on to roadway at Flash Gate. Left
then right at footpath sign, through stile by gate to enter field. On a right
diagonal, walk over to Ramsgreave Hall to enter farm trackway.*

Ramsgreave Hall

Ramsgreave is mentioned in the Domesday Book as a wood one league
square with an hawk's eyrie in it. Today only a small fragment of that once
great wood remains in the form of three small woods to the east of Hagg's
Hall.

Ramsgreave Hall to Saccary House

*Follow the farm road down, passing 'China Town' cottages to Hagg's Hall
farmyard. Pass through gate by higher stock shed and walk around to the
right to follow hedge-line around the corner down to old fence-line. From
here walk directly over to the left to pass over footbridge in hedge. Walk
directly on to enter lane above house via gate. Walk on to junction, then walk
up to the left a few paces to go over stile and stream on right (again we are
on the line of the Roman road and the paving can be observed in the banking). Walk on to the gateway above Midge Hall. From here walk up the field
on a slight right-diagonal to go over stile. Walk directly across the field to go
over footbridge down on left. Walk on and follow stream up to pass through
stile in hedge. Walk on and up to the left to pass through field-gate.*

*Walk on a few paces to pass over stone-stile on right into the grounds of
Saccary House. Walk down to go left at the covered well, up the steps and
along the path to pass over a footbridge onto roadway.*

Saccary House

SACCARY HOUSE

Saccary House is a late 17th century building, Ministry of Housing and Local Government listed. The outside of the house has little of its original character, being much altered and modernised. Inside, the central chimney opens onto the hall and kitchen, an arrangement from the early period. On walking through the gardens notice the half-sunken building which could be a covered well.

On Saccary Lane itself are a number of handloom weavers' cottages, numbers 1 to 7 being good examples. Handloom weaving thrived in Mellor during the 18th and 19th centuries when home life and industry went hand in hand. In 1770, William Radcliffe (known for his improvements to the power loom) noted that the land in Mellor was occupied by fifty to sixty farmers and of these only six or seven made a living primarily from farming. All the others got their income from some branch of trade, such as spinning and handloom weaving wool or cotton goods. Other good examples of weavers cottages can be seen on Barker Lane, Church Lane, Mellor Lane and in Mellor Brook.

Saccary House to Mellor Earthwork

Turn left then right at the last cottage to go over stile on banking. Follow right-hand fence to corner and on across to far corner of field to go through stone stile. Turn right and walk on to pass through stone gap-stile. Pass over stile opposite and walk up the field on a right diagonal to opposite corner to go over stile. Walk on up to the summit of Mellor Hill.

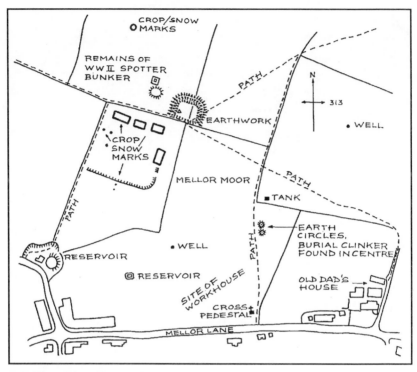

Mellor Earthwork

One local site that has drawn some attention over the recent years is the ancient
earthwork that stands above Ribchester on
the south bank of the Ribble near Mellor.
The site is in the centre of Mellor Moor,
upon the rounded top of the highest hill in
the neighbourhood; the sides of the hill
slope away gradually all round, making the
position an excellent one for a Roman signal
station, as has been suggested by many
writers.

The views on all sides are very extensive
and a finer spot for erecting a fortified post
could hardly be imagined.

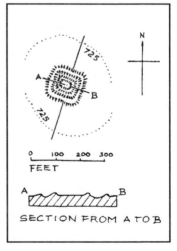

SECTION FROM A TO B

The earthwork is small, enclosing an oblong interior area only 60ft long by 35ft broad; this is raised about 3ft above the level of the adjoining ground. Around it is a rampart, once 2ft high, enclosed by a fosse about 5ft deep from its uppermost edge. Outside this is a second rampart, rising about 2ft higher than the ground outside. The inclusive measurements of the work and its defences are 130ft by 110ft, and the ground covered by it is about three-eighths of an acre.

An inscribed Roman altar, once sited in Samlesbury Hall but now lost, was found on Mellor Moor, leading some to suppose that a temple-type structure once stood here.

 A second Roman altar was found in 1988 by workmen cleaning out ditches and hedging. It has clear bolsters and a focus on top with a rudimentary pediment between them. The altar is cut from fine-grained sandstone and bears no inscription.

The place-name Mellor is a compound name, of which both elements are Celtic (British) meaning 'bare hill'. For something to be declared bare suggests that this was not always the case.

The parish of Mellor cum Eccleshill reflects a territorial layout dating back to pre-Conquest times; Blackburnshire was then organised on a Celtic territorial model — a central Caput (Whalley) between two Commotes (Whalley Parish, Blackburn Parish), each divided into multiple estates of two vills, arable land and summer pasture. Mellor with Eccleshill was one such multiple estate, Mellor being the estate lands and Eccleshill the upland pasture.

The place-name Eccleshill means 'the church hill'. This Celtic word is derived from a British form of Latin — Ecclesia — and implies the existence of some sort of Celtic population centre with organised worship.

In Lancashire we have five possible Romano-British Christian sites, Eccleshill in Blackburnshire being one of them. Apart from the name, we have no other firm evidence that an early church stood at Eccleshill. In fact, no archaeological evidence is at present available for any of the 'eccles' sites. Was Eccleshill the 'church hill' or was it the upland pasture of the 'church hill' being Mellor?

There is a tradition in the village of Mellor that a church, now said to be buried, stood on the top of Mellor Moor by the ancient earthwork. This area is locally known as 'Sod Huts'. Recent aerial photography has shown what could be a vallum and other structures near the earthwork. Also, according to Prior Wessington of Durham (1416), the body of St. Cuthbert was rested at Mellor and a chapel was dedicated to the Saint in the 9th century.

What, then, have we got at Mellor? A possible Roman fortification? A Romano-British population centre with organised worship? A Celtic monastic site? A 9th century church dedicated to St. Cuthbert? Without further archaeological investigation and closer inspection of past records and existing objects it is not practicable to form any firm conclusions at this stage.

The earliest 'mark of man' to come to light at Mellor was the discovery, in 1855, of an axe hammer of Langdale volcanic rock. The axe is polished and measures 8" long by 3" wide and there is a perforation near the flat head. The axe is now on view in Blackburn Museum.

STONE AXE HAMMER , MELLOR

The mediaeval tapestry of this delightful corner of the Ribble Valley is interwoven with many colourful events and persons, laced here and there with those darker threads of plague, warfare and religious suppression that together make up a local reflection of our Nation's history from the time of Domesday to the dawn of the Industrial Age. At each place of interest visited within the walks, these events and their effects will be unwoven in what remains in those surroundings to still catch the detecting eye.

The first shimmerings of light that were to break into the satanic dawn of industrialisation were first noticed in the early 16th century when the textile trade began its steady progress through east Lancashire. By 1700 each district was specialising in the production of one type of cloth more than another. The Preston area produced linen cloth, Blackburn was a centre for fustians, and up the Calder Valley woollens and worsteds were manufactured. As the century progressed it was witness to large increases in the production of cotton cloth. Between 1741 and 1750 Lancashire spinners and weavers doubled their annual consumption of raw cotton and by 1780 they had doubled it again. Nothing could retard this remarkable rate of development.

This growth led to colonies of handloom weavers being established throughout Lancashire, many on the edges of established rural settlements, whilst others brought new life to formerly declining villages. The village of Ribchester provides a good example of the latter. Surviving in Church Street and elsewhere are a few cottages showing the blocked-in remains of ground floor and cellar loomshops, again with triple windows.

The Mellor district provides many examples of the former. Colonies are to be found on Saccary lane, Whinney Lane, Barker Lane and Mellor Lane.

The remains of other industrial enterprises from this period are to be found in the many ruins of old bobbin mills in the surrounding districts. Cowley Brook, which runs through Dilworth Bottoms, has seven water-powered mills on its course from Knowle Green to Ribchester. Many others are to be found hidden in the deep ravines between Dutton and Hurst Green.

Looking at the location of these sites one can only marvel at the sheer tenacity and skills of the people who built and worked them in an age when mechanical aids were practically non-existent. Apart from constructing the buildings, weirs, lodges and dams, it was often necessary to build an access road to the nearest highway, which could be up to a mile away. The comb mill in Duddel Woods is an example of this.

With the introduction of the canal and rail network, we see the concentation of industries in the towns along their routes. The weavers of Mellor and Ribchester left their rural settings to join the ever-swelling sprawls of Blackburn and Preston.

Had the Leeds and Liverpool Canal followed its first intended course, from Chorley along the south bank of the Ribble to Whalley and on to Colne, the face of the Ribble Valley would be a far different one than it presents today.

Row after row of terraced housing would have reached up from the valley floor. The old halls and farmsteads we see today would have given way to the dark mill, its chimney dominating the parish church tower in praise of wealth over that of the Lord. We have much to thank for that turn of fate that has left the district for the most part unspoilt. The near landscape is most valuable and lovable, a treasured resource.

Mellor Earthwork to Village

Facing west at the triangulation point, follow fence on left to go over stile on left. Follow right-hand fence down, over stile and onto the roadway at Mellor.

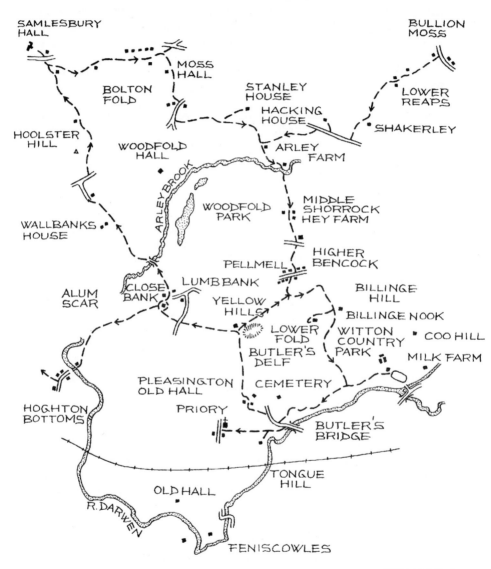

WALK No. 4

Walk 4

LAST MARTYR
TO
CROMWELL

Witton, Pleasington, Samlesbury & Billinge

8 miles, 4 hours

START: *Witton Park or Samlesbury Hall*

MAPS: *O.S. SD 62/72 & 63/73 PATHFINDER*

LUNCH: *Clog & Billycock*

On this walk we tread in the footfalls of a King on a visit to an Alum Mine, and a martyr who was to hang on Tyburn Tree.

We visit Witton Country Park, 224 acres that encompasses both man-made and natural scenery, historical features, informative nature trails and a visitors centre. The walk takes in seven major sites of historical and architectural note as well as others worth mentioning along the way.

So let us now be gone on this delightful and most rewarding walk over Blackburn's most dominant hilltops. The walk can also be linked to Walks 5 and 6 at Close Bank Farm.

Witton Park

Witton is made up of several old farmsteads — Billinge Nook on Under Billinge Lane, with an old well set in the wall opposite the farm. The Eyes (or Witton Ees) was a farm which stood on the site of Scapa weaving sheds. In 1404, Thomas Cowburne held the Eyes of Witton.

Coo Hill, meaning 'Cow Hill', is the site of a 16th century farm converted into dog kennels by the Fielden family in the 19th century, these can still be seen today along with some of the old farmhouse walls.

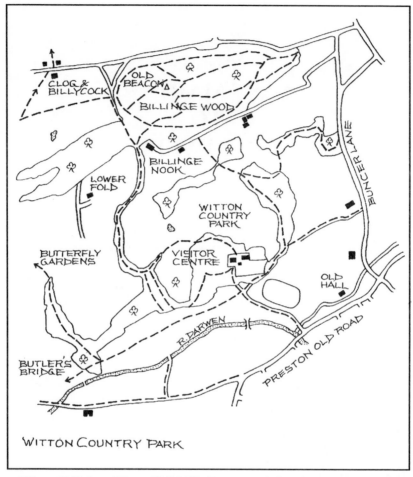

WITTON COUNTRY PARK

Witton Hall, later Witton Hall Milk Farm, stands in ruin on the edge of the allotments. Old mullioned windows lie in the weeds that now cover the site along with a large stone trough and an old well.

Reset into the low walls of the house is an old door lintel dated 1718 with the initials I.H.M. being those of John and Martha Holme. John Holme was Vicar of Blackburn from 1706 till his death in 1738. The Holdens were another well known family at Witton, they had been tenants here since before 1387.

In pre-Conquest times Witton formed a small multiple estate along with Billington. This is not so strange as it seems as Billinge and Billington have the same name origin.

WITTON OLD HALL

During the Late Bronze Age a tribe, known as the 'Billings' (folk of the sword) had a settlement upon these northern Blackburn Hills, a burial site of theirs can be seen at Hardmans Gap, Revidge.

Witton Country Park to Pleasington Hall

From the cafe follow the path along the edge of the wood, over stone footbridge and stile, then cross the field to go over a stile and footbridge. Cross the playing fields by the edge of the wood to the Cemetery driveway.

Walk up the driveway and turn left at the duck pond and walk on to the gateway. Turn right and walk past the new house and converted barn to the gate at Pleasington Old Hall.

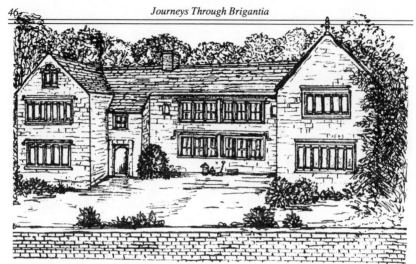

Pleasington Old Hall

In the time of King John, the manor of Pleasington was held of the Lord of Billington as one plough land. It formed part of the tenement which Efword de Billington, brother of Leofwin, Lord of Altham and Clayton-le-Moors, held in c.1160 in the time of Henry II.

In 1208, Elias de Billington, son of Efword, acknowledged in the Kings Court at Lancaster that the plough land in Pleasington and a small tenement in Billington were the right of Elias de Pleasington, son and heir of his brother Henry de Pleasington.

The manor passed by marriage to John de Winckley in c.1300. Agnes, the daughter (or granddaughter) of John de Winckley, married John, base son of Robert Ainsworth of Ainsworth in Middleton by Malbot de Crompton his concubine, and brought him by dowry the manor of Pleasington in c.1350.

The Ainsworths lived here for many years till Edward Ainsworth sold the manor to Richard Butler of Rawcliffe in 1777, two years before his death, he had no male issue.

The Hall is dated 1587, and above the doorway is a carved panel bearing the arms of the Ainsworth family with the in-

PLEASINGTON OLD HALL

itials of Thomas de Hoghton and John Southworth of Samlesbury, being the chief owners of land in Pleasington.

The building is on an H-plan, the centre hall has a six-light mullioned window on each floor with small flanking round-headed windows on the upper floor, and a two-storeyed lean-to porch with an old moulded doorway. The right wing has a fourteen-light mullioned window above. The left wing has a sash window on the ground floor, a six-light mullioned window on the first floor and a two-light mullioned window in the attic.

Inside the hall is a recess 12" x 15" and 2'6" from the floor, situated in the front wall at the south-west corner. It is known as the 'Priest Hole', and in the recess is fitted with an oak frame in which are cut the initials I.A., referring to John Ainsworth.

The Hall stands upon the site of a much earlier house of the 14th century, some of the remains of the moat can still be traced in the grounds of the house.

The 'White Lady' ghost that wanders the lanes around the Great Hall at Samlesbury is claimed by some to be Dorothy Winckley of Pleasington Hall. Dorothy married first a Southworth, then a de Hoghton, and finally Thomas Ainsworth, who later became a Protestant, or so the story goes.

Whatever the case, stories of the neverworld seem to be recalled far more often than fact, giving these old houses even more enchantment than they already possess.

Pleasington Hall to Close Bank Farm

Follow track left, through gate and up into the field. Head up to the top of the field, via three lone trees, to go over stile by gate. Follow path up to near edge of garden of Pleasington Old School House, turn left onto other pathway and walk down to go over stile. Following the old tree-line, cross the field to go through gateway, walk straight on to go over stile by gate. Follow track to road. Cross the road and go through the gateway into field. Follow right-hand hedge to Close Bank Farm and walk to the left, through gateway, along garden fence to stile by gate.

You can now go on to Alum Scar or join on to Walks 5 and 6 at Hoghton Bottoms to visit Hoghton Tower and return via Feniscowles or the Leeds and Liverpool Canal. The choice is entirely yours.

Close Bank to Hoghton Bottoms

Pass over the wall-stile at the side of the cattle grid and follow wall to go over next wall-stile. Follow right-hand hedgerow, on down the field, keeping to the left to go over stile in wall. Walk on down and up to follow edge of the wooded clough on down to the river. Follow track up to farm, over the stile and on through the garden to cross the footbridge into Hoghton Bottoms.

Close Bank to Alum Scar

Pass over stile and walk on to go down the farm lane, through gate, to go left down the old lane into Alum Scar. The mines are off the path over on the left, you may now explore these using the separate map given here. Otherwise you can go down to the bridge and follow the directions to Samlesbury Hall.

Alum Scar

Alum Crag is situated near the confluence of the Arley or Alum House Brook with the River Darwen. The Scar is composed of a thick stratum of aluminous shale. When mined it was used as an astringent and styptic employed by clothiers, glovers, dyers, etc.

The mine at Alum Scar was set up by Sir Richard Hoghton and proved to be a profitable venture for him. When James I visited Hoghton Tower in 1617, he was brought to look at the workings, as is mentioned in the Journal of Nicholas Assheton of Downham Hall:

"Aug. 16. Hoghton. The King Hunting: a great companie. Killed affore dinner a brace of stags. Verie hott;.... about 4 o'clock the King went down to the Allome mynes, and was ther an hower, and viewed the preciselie".

The Crown had a royalty upon the mine and, on October 22nd, Nicholas's Journal records: "my brother Anderton was at Hoghton upon a commission from the King to view the Allome mynes".

Later, these Alum works were held on joint lease from the Duchy of Lancaster by a Mr Ramsey and Lady Sarah Hoghton. In 1658, Lady Sarah entered into articles of agreement with Captain James Benson, Bailiff of Preston and a Parliamentarian during the Civil wars, to work her ladyship's portion of the mines.

Captain Benson's speculation proved ruinous, having his works seized by his creditors and himself imprisoned for debt. It seems that Lady Sarah had contrived with others to dupe Benson and bring about his downfall. Remember, they were on opposite sides during the Civil War and the reason for such a deed may well lie in these times. On his treatment by Lady Sarah, Benson declared that he had "received the hardest measure that ever a poor man received from any person professing truly to fear God" and vowed he "would never have any more to do with any business that concerned her ladyship's honour".

The working of the mine ceased after his failure, but the mine was reopened some time after by Sir E. Colebrooke, whose venture turned out no better than that of Bensons. Alum was mined only in a small way after these times, and all that remains of former enterprise is ruinous and overgrown. But the deer have returned to Alum Scar along with many other species of wildlife.

An Exploration of the Alum Workings

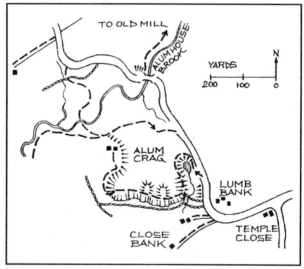

Walk down the old cobbled lane to go through the break in the left-hand wall above the water-filled hollow.

Follow the well defined path around the hollow to gain the embankment on the far side, follow the path on through the trees to arrive at the sharp ridge of bare grey shale which abuts against the rocks of Alum Scar. Descend the shale and traverse the over to the rock face. Cross the Crags from bay to bay to a series of small depressions.

At this point turn right and head down to find a well defined path running from east to west a few yards before Alum House Brook. Follow the path east to arrive back on the cobbled lane.

WOODFOLD HALL

Woodfold Hall

Overlooking this wooded district is the ruin of Woodfold Hall, a mansion built by the architect James Wyatt in 1798. Though now gutted, it still has its beautifully smoothly ashlared facade of nine bays with a portico of four giant unfluted columns with Adamish capitals.

Inside the grounds of Woodfold Park, for the most being private property, are two large lakes, an old saw mill and an ice house, one of the few remaining in Lancashire.

Near to the Hall, hidden by an overgrown copse, is a fine Victorian conservatory that is sadly falling to ruin. The Hall can be viewed from a distance with the use of field-glasses.

Alum Scar to Samlesbury Hall

Pass over the bridge and follow track up, through gate, then walk down the lane to the junction with Further Lane (Woodfold Hall can be seen on your right when walking down the lane). Turn right and walk on to go over stile by gate on the left. Follow track and right-hand hedge, over stile, and on to enter Hoolster Farm by farm gate. Right, then left, and follow farm lane down to Samlesbury Hall.

Samlesbury Hall

Samlesbury Hall is one of the most outstanding Lancashire Halls of the timber-framed variety. It belonged to the Southworth family from c.1330 till 1679, when they were forced by poverty to sell their holdings.

Originally the house was larger than it is now. The hall range formerly carried on and, at right angles to its end, the kitchen range ran east again, thus forming a courtyard with buildings on three sides. The hall is of the 15th century, and the long south range was added in c.1545. Much of the building was altered and restored in 1835.

The Hall's main feature is the polygonal bay window with its oblong upper part and gable, once used either to display the family plate or as the ladies bower. The stained glass heraldic devices were added in 1936, and depict ten Kings and Queens of England. The room above is known as the 'Priest's Room', after the small hiding hole built into the enclosed angle where the roof joins the main hall.

During the Reformation the Southworths refused to accept the demanded religious conformity of 1559. The Head of the family at that time was another Sir John Southworth, who even in these times, was appointed High Sheriff of Lancashire in 1561. Sir John even sat as an ecclesiastical commissioner, despite his opposition to the laws he was meant to be enforcing.

He was eventually dismissed and summoned to London to be questioned by Matthew Parker, the Archbishop of Canterbury. Unwilling to repent, the government gave up on him and Sir John was allowed to return to Samlesbury and begin again to lead a normal life, though a watchful eye was kept on him by the authorities.

All went well until the 1581 Act which made it treason to acknowledge the

Pope's authority in England. Sir John was one of the first to be caught in the web of suspicion. Fines and periods in prison were to follow, and faced with much debt and the possible forfeiture of his estates, he began to attend the local Protestant church.

This token act allowed his family to remain at Samlesbury and secretly keep the Catholic Faith. But the persecution never ended and he was hounded for his religious beliefs almost to the end of his life. He died, aged 69, on 3rd November 1595.

The Southworths came to Samlesbury when Gilbert de Southwort married Alice Deuyas. Her Father, Nicholas Deuyas, settled half of the manor of Samlesbury upon the couple. Gilbert at that time was High Sheriff of Lancashire (1325-1326), and his son, also called Gilbert, served for two years as Keeper of the Royal Forest.

All the Southworths were prominent knights, and several undertook military service, the most noted of these being John Southworth who served in France during Agincourt campaign.

During the Civil Wars the Southworth family remained Papists and suffered more fines on an already encumbered inheritance. By 1666 they had to mortgage Samlesbury Hall to pay of the many debts. Finally, Edward Southworth sold all their holdings in Samlesbury to Thomas Bradyll of Portfield, near Whalley, in 1679.

Given their strength of faith it is hardly surprising that a Southworth would eventually be martyred and later canonised for his religious beliefs.

St. John Southworth, nephew of old Sir John, became a priest at the Roman Catholic college of Douai in France in 1617. After working in London for several years, he was arrested and condemned to death in 1627.

For a time he was reprieved and heroically helped the people of London during the plague of 1636. He was finally arrested for preaching his faith and again sentenced to death. On 28th June 1654, he was executed at Tyburn — the last martyr to Catholicism under the rule of the Commonwealth.

By the early 1800's Samlesbury Hall had become a roadside inn, the Bradyll Arms and, after that, a girls' boarding school. Later the Hall was bought by Joseph Harrison who did much to restore the building. Sadly he later committed suicide over financial matters and the Hall was again plunged into uncertainty.

Eventually a Trust was established and the Hall was further restored and repaired. Today it has become one of the most important tourist attractions of the Ribble Valley.

To the right of the main entrance to the Hall stands a small Tudor-style lodge house. Not a building of any great importance you might think, in that you would be wrong. Set within its fabric is one of Blackburn's oldest fragments of history.

Built into the lower north wall are the last surviving remains of St. Mary's Parish Church that once stood in the now Cathedral grounds in Blackburn. These stones bear the date 1614, and the inscription pictured right.

FOUNDATION STONES
BLACKBURN
PARISH CHURCH

Another strange monument stands in a raised position by the side of the driveway. I am informed that it is part of an old sewerage or water conduit from Preston. The dedication on the plinth of the monument reads thus:

IN MEMORIAM G.H.J.HURST COLLEGH
REGALIS CANTABRIGIENSIS QUONDAM
SOCII PRO PATRIA MORTUI

and on the opposite side:

SIVE MITHRAS QUONDAM TE PERSICUS ENSE CECIDIT
SEU FABER EXCUDIT VENALI SERVICUS ARTE
OSTENDIS TAURUS VIM VIRTUTEMQUE VIRILEM

Samlesbury Hall to Stanley House

Walk back up the lane and take the left fork. Follow the lane up for nearly one mile, then turn right into Moss Hall driveway (last farm on right). Walk up the drive to gate.

Walk to the left to go around to the rear of the house. Walk on to pass through gateway and follow left-hand fence and stream up to pass through a small iron gate. Go around the house on the left to go through corner gate onto the road at Bolton Fold.

Turn right and walk along the road to Woodfold Park gates. Go through the gate on the left and follow track on to go over stile by gate. Follow hedge-side path to Stanley House, keeping the hedge on your right.

Stanley House

Stanley House was built in 1640. It is a large flat-fronted building with many mullioned windows of between three and six lights, and all have running mouldings above. The asymmetrical porch is a tall flat-topped structure that leads on to the large central chimney, and opens into the hall and kitchen. The second floor porch window is stepped with three lights.

The framed square above the doorway once held the datestone. For some reason this was removed some years ago and taken to the old saw-mill in Woodfold Park. Perhaps when the house is restored the stone will be re-set. Inside the house are two large inglenook fireplaces. What a warm place it must have been in those days, a far cry from the neglect of today.

Stanley House appears to have been, for a long period, the reputed manor house of Mellor. During the 16th century it was the property of the Stanley family. Later, in the second half of the 17th century, the Yates family made it their seat.

On the Yates' Map of 1786, Stanley House is shown to have a tree-lined driveway leading to it. This runs up from near Arley Fold, and sections can still be made out today. The lower part of its length is included within this walk.

Stanley House to Clog and Billycock

Walk back along the hedgerow to the gate. Follow wall to go over the stile on the left into the field. Follow right-hand fence down to go over fence-stile onto trackway. Walk down the trackway, across the lane, on and over stile.

Follow left-hand hedge, past the cottage, and on to go over stile by gate. Left, following old trackway, over footbridge and on to farm wall. Follow wall down, through gate, and over stream by stepping-stones.

Follow left-hand fence up the hill to go over stile by gate and on up to Middle Shorrock Hey (notice the three-light mullioned window on the side of the house). Walk up the lane to the junction with Meins Road, and through the gateway opposite. Follow the old trackway up and onto the road.

Shorrock Hey and Higher Bencock

Shorrock Hey is a very ancient farmstead. The land hereabouts was settled upon Margaret, daughter of John Shorrock, in 1336. The present farmhouse at Middle Shorrock Hey was built in the 17th century, but little of the original building remains today. On the side of the house can be seen a lone mullioned window from that early building.

At Bencock stands the Clog and Billycock Inn. A strange name, said to be taken from an earlier landlord who sported such attire. His likeness can be seen on the pub's sign.

THE CLOG & BILLYCOCK

The Inn serves very good ale and bar meals are available during the day, the latter being excellent value for such good food.

Across the way, built into the front of a house, is a stone head of a man who bears a strong likeness to Oliver Cromwell.

Billing Nook Farm

Clog and Billycock to Witton Country Park

Walk down past the pub and left over stile after car park. Follow trackway up to go over stile. Follow left-hand fence to go over stile on the left. Walk across the field to the picnic area gate. Follow the wall down the hillside to the lane (Haydock Fold, a 17th century farmhouse is down to the right). Pass over the cattle-grid, right, over the stile and follow the path down to Witton Park.

The map of Witton Country Park indicates the number of walks that can be had in Witton Country Park. All the farmsteads are working farms so respect their livelihood and keep to the well marked and defined pathways.

Walks around Billinge and the Yellow Hills are especially pleasing on a fine evening when you can watch the sunset over the Irish Sea, a moment for reflection before turning once again to the grey sprawl of Blackburn and its environs.

To walk the hills so near this town,
To pass again the place where younger I did play,
To see no change to all around,
That is a good and pleasant day.

Journeys Through Brigantia

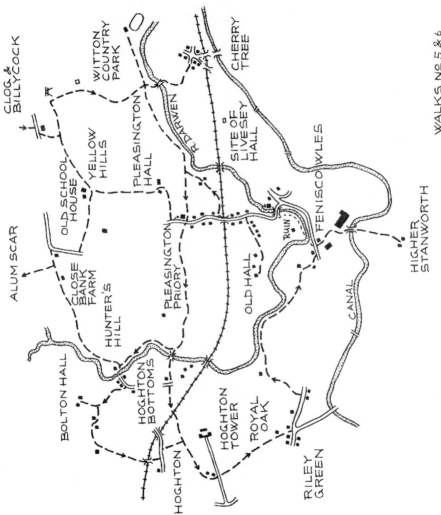

WALKS No 5 & 6

Walks 5 & 6
HOGHTON BOTTOMS
AND
THE YELLOW HILLS

Witton Park, Pleasington, Hoghton,
Riley Green & Cherry Tree

8 and 5 miles

START:	*Witton Park, Hoghton Tower or Pleasington Priory*
MAP:	*O.S. SD 62/72 PATHFINDER*
LUNCH:	*Royal Oak, Clog & Billycock or Butlers Arms*

These two walks offer a combination of many other short or longer walks over a varied and interesting landscape. Both walks start at Witton Park Visitors Centre, but you can just as easily start them anywhere along the route. Walk 5 goes through to Hoghton Tower to return via Pleasington or the Leeds and Liverpool Canal. Walk 6 goes down into Hoghton Bottoms and returns over the Yellow Hills to Witton.

Witton Country Park

Witton is an old Anglo-Celtic settlement, the arable land in a multiple estate with Billington, the latter being the summer pasture. The derivation of the name being 'Witta's Tun', Witta being an Old English name of common use. The estate is first mentioned in the Lancashire Assize Rolls of 1246.

In 1340, Adam de Radcliffe held Witton of Queen Isabella by knights service. Sometime during 1345, Adam was declared an outlaw for felony at Lancaster Castle for his burning of the houses of John de Pudsey. But anticipating trouble Adam had previously enfeoffed the vicars of Whalley and Blackburn of his estate at Witton, and they, obtaining Royal Assent, alienated it in 1347 to the Abbey and Convent of Whalley.

The demesne of Witton continued in the hands of the monks of Whalley until the dissolution of the Abbey.

Witton was then sold to Richard Crombelholme of Dutton in 1544. Four days later it was conveyed to George Astley of Stakes in Bowland in whose line it continued until the late 17th century. Years later it was acquired by Joseph Fielden of Blackburn in 1788.

Today, Witton is a delightful Country Park with many fine attractions. A Visitors Centre has been developed from the Fielden Coach House and Stables, once part of the now-demolished Witton House. The facilities at the centre include stables, harness room and coach house with displays of harness, farm tools, horse-drawn farm machinery and several horse-drawn carriages.

The Natural History Room displays the wildlife to be found on the many nature trails within the Park. Also included is a lecture room and changing exhibitions are held there. Sports facilities are also numbered among the Park's attractions.

Witton Park to Pleasington Priory

From the cafe follow the path along the edge of the wood, over stone footbridge and stile, then cross the field to go over stile and footbridge. Cross the playing fields to go up the sandy path to the Butlers Arms.

Pleasington Priory

The Roman Catholic church of St Mary & John the Baptist, known locally as Pleasington Priory, affords a proud landmark in the red and gold rays of the setting sun over the playing fields.

The church was built in the years 1816-1819 as a thanks-offering of John Francis Butler of Pleasington Hall.

According to tradition, John had met with a serious accident while hunting on the site of the present church and was very nearly killed. He there and then resolved to erect a church on the very spot in thanksgiving for his fortunate escape.

Considering that it was built before the Act of Catholic Emancipation in 1829, it is an astonishing edifice, large and, though without a tower, very prominent on its site. The frontage was modelled on that of Whalley Abbey before the Dissolution.

This was the Parish Church of my younger years. As a family we would catch the Ribble Sunday special to Pleasington along with others in those days of few motor cars. On entering the churchyard one could not help looking up with a sense of awe at the giant rose window flanked by two tall pinnacles. The eyes would then drop to the statues of Saints and the grotesque carved heads above the front doorway.

Inside one was greeted by the smell of candle wax and incense, then from that Gothic pile would come the cold damp that seemed to fall from the rib-vaulted aisles to meet that rising from the stone flagged floor. As the Latin was chanted, and the sunlight caught the figures depicted in the stained-glass windows, one was overcome by the mediaeval setting, suggesting worship from that first dawn of Light on Celtic Britain.

BUTLERS ARMS

Pleasington is the site of the ancient 'Pleasa's tun', an even earlier settlement than Blackburn. During the 14th century, Sir Robert de Pleasington
(died 1393), who belonged to the family who took their name from here, was
Chief Baron of the Exchequer.

Standing opposite the Priory is the Butlers Arms. Built in the Gothic Style,
its frontage blends in well with the setting. The Inn boasts a fine bowling
green and beer garden adding pleasure to a summer's evening aided by a few
jugs of Old Peculier.

Butlers Arms to Hoghton Bottoms
and Hoghton Tower

*Follow track to the right of pub to go over stile. Over the hill, following
left-hand fence, over two stiles, down to go over wall stile. Follow right-hand
wall to go over stile and on down to river bridge. (From here we can go on up
to the Tower or follow the river down to cross into Hoghton Bottoms and visit
Bolton Hall.)*

*Cross the bridge and walk up the lane to roadway. Right, and over stile on
left to follow path up to cross the railway. Follow the path to the right to go
over stile. Follow wall round, over stiles, to the Tower driveway.*

To Hoghton Bottoms and Bolton Hall

*Walk down the right-hand bank of the river to the ford. Cross by way of
footbridge and walk into the hamlet.*

Hoghton Bottoms

Thirty years ago Hoghton Bottoms was a much frequented place, tea was served by a local farmer's wife and the old mill still had its water wheel. Today the hamlet has few visitors, the water wheel has gone and the mill stands as a relic to unwise conversion.

A walk along the mill-race, through the gorge with its towering railway arches, up as far as the weir is most rewarding. Wild garlic covers the ground and broadleafs fall to meet the river. All in all, a very restful setting.

Hoghton Bottoms to Bolton Hall

After the last cottage on the right, on corner of bend, turn right up track, over stile and right, down the side of the cottage and on to go over stile. Follow path to overhead cables. Follow overhead cables up the hill, over the stile and onto the road. Turn right and walk on to Bolton Hall.

Bolton Hall

The tiny Jacobean farmhouse of Bolton Hall stands on a rise between Wild Bottom's Wood and the riverside hamlet of Hoghton Bottoms. The house is in very good order with a fine front garden to match. The roof is stone tiled and the windows are mullioned — three-light mostly with whitewashed stones and a small porch set into the south front.

Bolton Hall to Hoghton Tower

Walk back along the lane to go right at fork, up Highfields Farm drive. Walk up and into the farmyard, past the hen cabins and on into field. Turn left, and keeping the hedge to your left, walk down to go over footbridge at 'T' in hedges. Follow hedge to the ruin of Tewit Hall. Follow trackway on, over railway, and on to the road. Turn left and walk on to go over stile on the right near gate. Follow hedge up to wood. Go over stile and follow wall-side path along and on to the Tower Driveway. Walk up to the Tower (if open).

Hoghton Tower

This large and spectacular castellated stone mansion stands upon a spur of hill overlooking the township of Hoghton in Gunnolfsmoors — a Hiberno-Norse settlement within the Leyland Hundred.

The mansion was built by Thomas Hoghton in the late 16th century. Thomas, a strong Catholic, unwilling to embrace the Protestant faith sought refuge in France never to see his great enterprise again. He died at Liege and was buried at Douai in 1580.

The Hoghton family, one of Lancashire's oldest and most famous and infamous, can trace their ancestry back to Hamon le Boteler who married a daughter of Warine Bussel, Norman Baron of Penwortham and holder of large estates in Lancashire.

The highlight of the family's history came in 1617 with the Knighting of 'Sir Loin' by King James I on a visit to Sir Richard Hoghton, High Sheriff of Lancashire, known at court by the title of 'Honest Dick'.

HOGHTON TOWER   HOGHTON TOWER

Sir Richard's son, Gilbert, also rode into the pages of history with his ill-fated assault on Blackburn during the Civil War. This led to the sequestering of his estates in 1646.

However his son, another Richard, was a strong supporter of Cromwell and the estate was returned to the family, the descendants of whom still live on the estate today.

The Tower has only seen action once, leading to its fall and capture by local Parliamentarians. During February 1643, a force of some three hundred men under the leadership of Captain Starkie of Huntroyde, were sent to take Hoghton Tower which was "fortified with three great pieces of ordnance, and some say with betwixt thirty and forty musketeers and some say more". After half an hour of consideration the place was surrendered upon quarter.

While Captain Starkie was searching the Tower for powder and arms an explosion took place. He and a number of his company were killed and others maimed. The explosion was due to the carelessness of one of his own men, but at the time was attributed to the malice of the defenders.

The Tower is open to the public: Easter Saturday, Sunday and Monday 14.00-17.00; every Sunday till the end of October; Saturday, Sunday, July, August and Bank Holidays. There is an admission charge.

Hoghton Tower to Riley Green

Walk back down the driveway to the lodge house, turn left and go through kissing-gate. Follow left-hand fence up to go over stile, and on over next stile. Walk down the field directly, over stile, straight down and over stile into farm lane. Walk on to Riley Green.

Riley Green

Time now for a welcome drink before we turn once again towards Blackburn. And we would have to travel far to come across a finer wayside inn than the Royal Oak. Notice the pub sign — the King is hiding inside the oak's green leaves, thus evading his Roundhead foe.

With the inn's whitened frontage and blackened corner stones it cannot help but bring back memories of the coaching days of old. Inside, beneath the low beamed ceiling, you will find many a cosy nook in which to rest, chat and enjoy good ale.

Down the road from Riley Green stands Causeway Farm, named after an ancient raised trackway that ran down through the wood to ford the river Darwen below Lodge Farm, we lose it on the golf course, but it can be made out again climbing Woodcock Hill as it crosses Long Lane.

With no mention on any known map, it has caused many to refer to it as the 'Old Roman Road'. Roman or not it remains one of the many local mysteries that abound in the district.

(If so wished you can now return to Witton via the canal to Cherry Tree and visit Stanworth Farm on the way, or simply walk along the canal to visit Stanworth and rejoin the walk at Feniscowles).

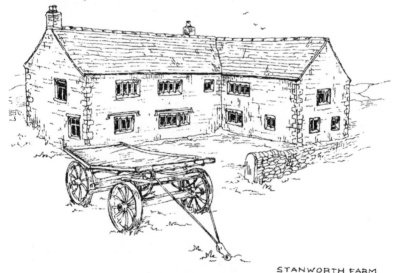

STANWORTH FARM

Riley Green to Feniscowles via Stanworth

Walk down the road and on to the canal tow-path at the boatyard. At the third bridge leave the canal and walk up to the 17th century farmstead of Stanworth with its fine farmhouse and barn. Return back over the canal to go on through the paper mill yard to the roadway to rejoin the walk.

Riley Green to Feniscowles Old Hall

Walk down the road, past Jackson Farm (dated 1799 J J Jackson), to turn left into gateway opposite red-brick house. Walk down track to go over stile by gate near house entrance. Follow track down to the river. Follow path up river to go over stile into wood. Follow path up and out of the wood, via stile. Cross field on a left diagonal to go over stile at 'T' in fences. Walk on to go over stile on right and cross the field on a left diagonal to enter lane by stile. Walk down to the road, turn left and walk on to go left down the road to Pleasington. Walk on to the edge of the village and go left down the first lane on the left. The Old Hall is at the very end of the lane.

Feniscowles Old Hall

Feniscowles is on the Darwen near its confluence with the Roddlesworth. The low ground near the river may have given rise to its name. Feniscowles is a partly Old Norse place-name and means 'muddy huts'.

The Old Hall is finely situated on a high bank overlooking the river, and is a two-story stone-built house of the 18th century. The principal front facing south has two gables and a projecting porch.

The building, which is now divided into two dwellings, has little architectural merit except for an ornamental plaster panel in one of the bedrooms with the initials of Thomas and Alice Livesey and the date 1726, and an old stone now used as a hearth-stone with the initials I.L.E. and the date 1709.

FENISCOWLES OLD HALL

Set in the wall of the barn is a sculptured door lintel bearing the initials T.L. A.L., and the date 1732, together with the initials I.L. (John Livesey).

The Hall was rebuilt after a fire in 1732 by Thomas and Alice Livesey. The original building, I am informed by the present owner, was a timber framed structure. The fireplace from this earlier building is still used, and a thirty foot deep well at the rear of the building is still in good order.

The Livesey family are recorded as living here as far back as 1404, when one Thomas de Livesey de Fenischales occurs. This yeoman family was a branch of Livesey, lords of Livesey cum Tocholes, whose family seat was Livesey Hall.

The old ruin that stands opposite the paper mills, on the north bank of the Darwen, is all that remains of Feniscowles New Hall. Built in 1808 by the factory owner William Fielden, it once stood in ornamental parkland populated by a herd of red deer. Imported from the Highlands by this fanciful gent, they would roam up the Roddlesworth to his lands beyond.

Dressed in the garb of a Highland chieftain, complete with battle axe, William must have cut a ludicrous figure strutting around his glen. What laughs the local farmers must have had when observing this romantic fool.

Feniscowles Old Hall to Tongue Hill

Walk back to the road and turn left into the village. Once over the railway bridge turn right, through gate, and along railway path to go through next gate. On a right diagonal, walk on to Tongue Hill, over stile and into the farmyard.

Tongue Hill

Another Old Norse name meaning 'spit of land', an apt description of this land thrust between Feniscowles and Pleasington.

Tongue Hill farm house stands in a very prominent position within a walled garden surrounded by a cobbled yard. The house is dated 1735 with the initials R.P.E.

The front has an asymmetrical facade on the pattern of the mediaeval hall and hall doorway arrangement. All the windows have chamfered mullions and there is a string-course above the ground floor windows and doorway. The side and rear of the house display work from the 17th

TONGUE HILL

century, and a close look at the front of the house will show the 18th century re-styling of the earlier facade. The builder of the house, before the front was altered, was Giles Cunliffe who lived here from 1619 to 1675. Giles was the grandson of Thomas Cunliffe of Pleasington who died in c.1611.

In 1328 it was recorded that John, son of Elias de Tong, gave the water mill at Pleasington to his brother Alexander in marriage with Alice, daughter of John de Hoghton. Their descendant, Katherine Tong, wife of John Seed of Ribchester, gave the estate in 1426/7 to William Seed. In 1457/8 Thomas Seed of Pleasington gave his lands and the mill to Richard Hoghton.

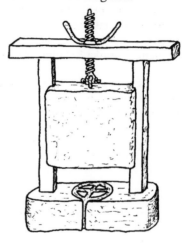

The mill later passed to the Southworths and then to the Liveseys. The water mill stood downriver from Tongue Hill and the remains of the mill race can still be made out today. In its time it was known as Tong Mylne and later Seed Mylne.

The old 17th century cheese press, pictured here, was found some years ago in one of the old outbuildings at Tongue Hill. It is now on public display in Blackburn Museum. Remains of another cheese press stands to the left of the walled garden in the farmyard.

Across the river, on the edge of the new estate, once stood Livesey Hall. Before it was demolished in the 1960s it was the most noted yeoman mansion

Livesey Hall

within North Lancashire. It had a large centre hall, with a gabled entrance porch and two end wings on the E-plan. All the windows were mullioned with hood-moulding except for the hall window which had a transom as well. The first floor of the porch was mullioned entirely: three lights to the sides, five lights to the front.

The house had three datestones, the one of 1605 referred to the majority of the building. 1666 came with the construction of the right wing. The date of 1689 was for internal work.

Two mullioned windows and the chimneys from the old hall are now incorporated into the renovated gatehouse at Martholme, Great Harwood. Even after demolition, these proud stones still have a role to play, giving strength and order to failing ancient piles.

Livesey is a most ancient township whose origins go back to the Dark Ages. Along with Tockholes, it formed a small multiple estate within the old Celtic Realm of Blackburnshire.

The place-name Livesey means 'to tower above, to stand out prominently' — this could possibly refer to Bunker's Hill, a prominent hill on the south west of Blackburn on which in Iron Age times stood a Celtic temple.

As a surname, Livesey is one of the oldest in Lancashire. Locally most of the family were farmers or builders in stone — Hacking Hall on the banks of the Ribble and Pleasington Priory are testament to their skill.

Tongue Hill to Witton

Pass through the gate and follow the track down into the playing fields. Walk through the fields back to Witton Country Park.

To those not familiar with the Darwen Valley this walk will have come as a pleasant surprise. The area of Hoghton Bottoms offers a variety of diverse walks and I suspect that you will return here many, many times.

Who knows — the farmer's wife may start serving teas again!

O ruins are lovely when o'er them is cast
The green veil of ivy to shadow the past;
When the rent and the chasm that fearfully yawn'd
By the moss of the lichens are sweetly adorn'd.

Walk 6

Follow Walk 5 description to the ford at Hoghton Bottoms.

Hoghton Bottoms to Close Bank Farm

At the ford go up past the front of the farmhouse on your left to go over a stile at the rear of the house. Walk on to follow trackway to go over stile. Follow edge of wood up and down to cross the clough. Walk up the bank on the right to go over wall stile. Walk on across the field to Close Bank Farm. Over the wall stile on left on gate and on over next wall-stile onto driveway.

Close Bank Farm

Close Bank Farm is a late 18th century building of some interest. Finial stone balls rest on each corner of the house, and beneath the gutter on the front elevation is a datestone of 1789, with the initials C.M.
(It is possible now to link onto Walk 5 and visit the Alum Mines and Samlesbury Hall to return back via Stanley House to Witton Park).

Close Bank to the Yellow Hills

Pass over stile opposite and around the garden fence to go through hedgerow. Follow hedgerow around to the road. Go through the gateway opposite and follow track and left-hand hedgerow on, through gateway and on to go over stile. On, following line of trees to go over stile. Follow pathway up to front of Old School House. Follow the path up on the right to go over stile. Walk up the field to go over stile and on up the hill to gain a terrific vantage point.

The Yellow Hills

The Yellow Hills take their name from the moorland grasses that grow around its tops that, viewed from afar, are always yellow in hue. From the top of this quarry delph we have excellent views over the Ribble Valley and Bowland Fells to the Lancashire coast with the Cumbrian hills to the north-west and the Welsh hills to the south-west. To the south the West Pennine Moors and the Rosendales are laid out before us in all their glory.

Yellow Hills to Clog & Billycock & Witton Park

Go down over the stile on your left to follow the track to the Clog & Billycock. Or alternatively: Follow path to go over stile and on across the field to enter picnic area via stile. Follow the paths (see Map Page 44) to the Visitors Centre.

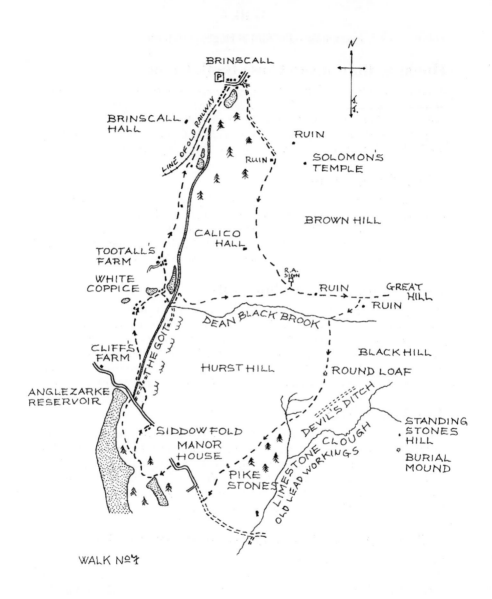

N

BRINSCALL

BRINSCALL
HALL

LINE OF OLD RAILWAY

RUIN

RUIN

SOLOMON'S
TEMPLE

BROWN HILL

CALICO
HALL

TOOTALL'S
FARM

WHITE
COPPICE

R.A.
SIGN

RUIN

GREAT
HILL

RUIN

DEAN BLACK BROOK

THE GOIT

CLIFF'S
FARM

BLACK HILL

HURST HILL

ROUND LOAF

ANGLEZARKE
RESERVOIR

DEVIL'S DITCH

STANDING
STONES
HILL

SIDDOW FOLD
MANOR
HOUSE

LIMESTONE CLOUGH
OLD LEAD WORKINGS

BURIAL
MOUND

PIKE
STONES

WALK No 7

Walk 7

THE ANCIENTS
LOOK DOWN

Brinscall, Round Loaf, Pikestones,
White Coppice

9 & 5 miles, 6 & 3 hours respectively

START: *Brinscall or White Coppice*

MAPS: *O.S. SD 62/72 & 61/71*

LUNCH: *Packed lunch and flask*

This walk climbs steeply from the village of Brinscall and skirts Brown Hill to enter the enchanted valley of Dean Black.

On the distant skyline Round Loaf invites us and, on ascending Black Hill, the views one gets from this friendly mound are magnificent, even though the peat blanket hides its ancient secrets.

On past the old lead workings to view Lancashire's most ancient monument, the first known resting place of man in the region.

From the moorland heights we quickly descend into a rolling green and rural landscape which culminates in the tranquil beauty of the tiny hamlet of White Coppice. On a summer's day, the lark's song is only broken by the sound of leather on willow.

We leave this paradise behind us to wend our way through leafy lanes, long ago abandoned by the rustic traffic, to reach water's edge and Brinscall once again.

As can be seen from the map, this ramble can be taken as one or two shorter walks. For the long walk we suggest Brinscall as your starting point; for the two shorter ones, White Coppice.

Brinscall to Round Loaf via Great Hill

*Cross the goit bridge at the junction of railway Road and School Lane to take
the narrow lane on the right that leads up to the moors. At the very top of the
lane we pass over a stile by a gate and take the track on the right that leads
us over the moors and round into Dean Black Valley. Walk on to meet with a
path coming up from the lower valley.*

*Here you will notice a metal footpath indicator plate, erected by the
Ramblers Association in 1963. Continue directly on the stile below Great
Hill. Walk down to the right to a ruin. from here a good path leads down the
valley to the tree-edged stream. Cross the stream to find a wide path that
leads directly up to Round Loaf.*

Round Loaf Tumulus

Round Loaf is the local name given to the round cairn or bowl barrow that
stands in a conspicuous position on the side of Black Hill Upper. The mound
is slightly elongated, measuring about 50 metres north to south and 45 metres
east to west.

In the summit of the mound is a small disturbance hollow caused by local
'flint' seekers. Now that the site is a Scheduled Ancient Monument it is
hoped that this type of robbery will cease.

The mound shows no traces of an outer ditch which has led some to
suggest a possible glacial origin. Only further archaeological investigation
will determine the true nature of the mound.

Whatever the origin of the cairn, it provides a good resting spot giving
excellent views of the surrounding moorland landscape.

Devil's Ditch

Devil's Ditch was constructed in the 18th century as part of the lead mining
complex on Anglezarke Moor. Its purpose was to give a greater force of water
to Limestone Brook which fed the waterwheel pit further down Limestone
Clough.

The earliest record of lead mining on Anglezarke is from 1692 when Sir
Richard Standish of Duxbury, the then landowner, signed an agreement with
Peter Shaw of Rivington and others to extract and process the lead ore. The
mines were worked off and on until 1837 from which time they fell into ruin.

The shafts were filled in in the 1950's to provide work for the unemployed people of Chorley. Since 1982 some of the remaining features, the slime and waterwheel pits, have been partially excavated by today's unemployed under the direction of various government agencies.

Round Loaf to Pikestones

Many paths lead away from Round Loaf, the one we take leads over to the south west to cross a stream and then we make our way to the top edge of the pine plantation. Follow the plantation fence on to pass over a stile onto the Pikestones.

THE PIKESTONES

The Pikestones, Anglezarke NGR 627172

'The Pikestones' is the local name given to a group of stones on Anglezarke Moor which are in fact the remains of a Megalithic chambered tomb, the only one known to exist in Lancashire.

Today, this badly robbed and ruined long cairn consists of the remains of a rectangular chamber, possibly divided into two compartments set towards the northern end of an elongated cairn of small stones partly covered with peat and grass.

The alignment is north-south, measuring about 150 feet long, 62 feet wide at the northern end and 45 feet at the southern end. There is no retaining kerb but some of the perimeter stones are somewhat larger than the stones of the cairn.

Of the chamber itself, two stones at the eastern end remain upright and a west side-stone leans against them. Behind these are two fallen stones which were once roof-stone and back-stone respectively, the latter having fallen outwards.

Three small stones are set across the northern end and it has been suggested that these may have acted as a sill dividing the 14-foot long chamber into two.

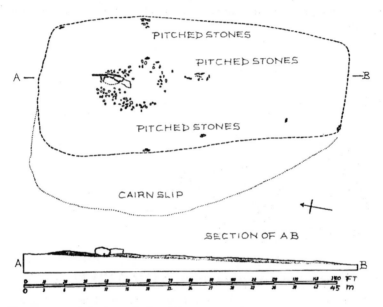

The true ground plan of The Pikestones has been the subject of two archaeological surveys: Dr J. D. Bu'lock (TLCAS. Vol. LXVIII. 1958) and Frances Lynch (PPS. Vol. XXXII. 1966) respectively.

Both survey drawings are reproduced here, but I consider each fall short of the true form and present layout of the monument. I take this view from my own close inspection of the site that has shown inconsistences and omissions in both surveys.

What is needed is a systematic geophysical survey and an analysis of the computer data — a worthwhile task for the newly formed Central Lancashire Archaeological Research Unit.

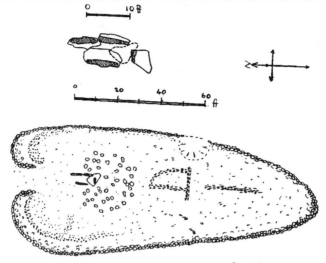

from Bullock

This Megalithic structure represents a zenith in the social structure of Neolithic society in Lancashire. The building of such a large monument would have consumed an appreciable share of the community's energy budget. Its construction and use would, to some extent, have performed a communal function, although it probably concealed the power of a small elite.

The tomb is built on the edge of the then settled landscape — The Lancashire Neolithic Floor. This floor is today preserved in the peat deposits of our upland moors.

The mean temperature was 2°C higher than it is today. This allowed expansion of agriculture and settlement to maximum elevations. They worked the lighter, higher soils as they did not have the technological force to exploit and clear the dense forests or till the heavy clay of the poorly drained valley floors, although recent practical experiments in Scandinavia and elsewhere have suggested that the humble stone axe, which is found in large numbers throughout the country, was a formidable tool which was capable of felling even fairly substantial hardwoods.

As the climate became cooler and wetter, in combination with the artificial clearance of forest in the upland areas leading to a gradual leaching of soil nutrients, sphagnum moss and cotton grass colonized the uplands resulting in the blanket of peat bog which is so widespread today.

This combination of factors led Neolithic man from his upland settlements down to the lower levels, a process that would only become complete in the Late Bronze Age.

This type of tomb does not represent the sole burial site of one person but of many persons over a period of time, and not always the full skeleton was interred in the chamber.

Evidence from other sites shows four major patterns: contrasts between articulated and disarticulated skeletons; others between immature and adult individuals; different treatment of male and female burials and a distinction between the left- and right-hand sides of the body.

Some have suggested that these arrangements are an assertion of the collective and a denial of the individual and of differences between individuals. An interesting theory, but I think that the true reason for such arrangements lies in the ways that bodies were stripped of flesh in the mortuary enclosures.

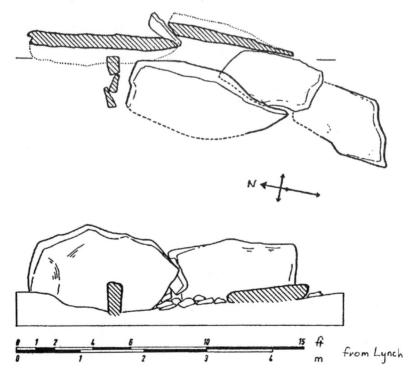

from Lynch

Many other chambered tombs await discovery in the Lancashire region and probable structures have been located in the Bowland and Rossendale districts. If all or most of the Megalithic structures could be located in the region we may then gain some knowledge of territorial divisions in Neolithic times.

It is conceivable that in the Atlantic facade that Lancashire then belonged that swidden agriculture was practised — the village would remain in one place for a decade or so and then, as the land nearby became exhausted, move on to new land in the same territory.

The tomb, or some other monument, would provide a territorial foci point for that family group, an enduring symbol of the continuity of their occupation of the land.

Each group would probably have consisted of around thirty persons — a single farming family, belonging to a larger folk/clan spread throughout the region, each group holding one territory, served by one tomb.

The building of Pikestones would take the twenty or so able-bodied inhabitants of 'Anglezark Territory' over thirty days. Such an investment of labour would have to be made over a number of years, and at times when there was little farming activity.

It is reasonable to suppose that they used the labour potential availability of neighbouring groups to join in the construction work. Given a suitable incentive — a great feast with amusement and exchanges providing a forum for social intercourse — co-operative effort can work to build impressive monuments.

Pikestones, along with other collective burial monuments, reflects the importance of the social occasion and the passionate concern for group status in Neolithic society. It would become the principle feature of the territory, which may itself have been known by the name of the monument. Its construction would be one of the steps such a group would have to take in order to establish its identity within the regional clan.

On returning to the Pikestones in July 1993 I noticed with disgust that some idiots have made a circle of stones around the chamber — a foolish act. These stones will be removed but the vandalous act of carving a tailed-spiral onto the cap-stone cannot be removed. Those responsible for this sacrilegious act gain our scorn — may the sky fall in on them for such a violation.

Pikestones to Manor House

*Walk down the edge of the plantation to the Jepson's Gate track via stiles.
(The way to the left leads to the start of the Leadmines Clough walk). The
track to the right leads to the road that leads on and down to the Manor
House —first house on the right.*

MANOR HOUSE

Manor House

Manor House, or High Bullough as it was once known, stands in a command-
ing position aside the Anglezarke road.

The house bears three date stones, 1604 R.S., 1620 and 1779, the former
relating to the Shaw family. John Shaw of High Bullough was a great
benefactor of Rivington Church, where his name appears on a memorial
brass.

Manor House to Siddow Fold

*Pass through the kissing gate by the road in front of the house and cross
the field directly to pass through gate. The path leads down to go over a
footbridge and on to another footbridge (do not pass over) to turn right at
crossing pathways.*

*Walk on to go over a stile, on, over a footbridge. Walk on to leave the path
by an old hollow-way that leads up to the right. Pass through a gate and
follow fence on right to the road at Siddow Fold.*

SIDDOW FOLD

Siddow Fold

Siddow Fold, now named Gamekeeper's Cottage, is an attractive Jacobean cottage with a whitewashed front. A fine reminder of an age gone by. The door lintel bears the date 1707 with the initials I.N., those of John Newton, a preacher at Rivington.

SIDDOW FOLD

Siddow Fold to White Coppice

Walk down the road to go through a gate on the right. (If you wish to visit Cliff's Farm, continue along the road to the first house on the right).

Follow track to go over a stile and a bridge on the left. Follow right-hand wall to go over a stile. Walk up the field on a slight left diagonal to go over a stile by a gate. Follow left-hand wall to go over a stile.

Follow trackway to White Coppice Farm. Walk down the farm lane to turn left into White Coppice.

Cliff's Farm

With round-headed and straight-headed windows to the front, Cliff's presents an interesting face to the inquiring eye. Cliff's is dated 1696, with the initials T.A. & R.M. with a single M above.

White Coppice

The tiny hamlet of White Coppice grew up around Alfred Eccles' weaving mill. The mill has been long demolished; all that remains of it today is the lodge, now a favourite haunt of fishermen.

Eccles was a firm advocate of temperence in drinking and smoking and devoted much energy and wealth to its advancement. Even today there is no watering hole in the village.

There are many 18th century cottages to be found in the village, those in The Row being good examples. What was once the village green is now a picturesque cricket field, and on a lazy summer's day it affords a favourite picnic spot with room for children to play amid delightful surroundings.

White Coppice to Brinscall

Walk back to White Coppice Farm and on along the lane to the cricket field. Walk along the edge of the cricket field to go up to the left behind the last white cottage. After passing through stile and gate take the path up the hillside that leads us on to Tootall's Farm via gate. Walk past the houses and barn to follow a path on the right.

After passing over the stile, continue on along the overgrown trackway to pass over a stile. Cross the field to corner of far fence. Follow fence on to pass through gate onto a lane by houses. Walk down the lane to pass through a kissing gate and cross the field directly to pass over stile. Walk on to pass over stile and flat-bridge. Follow path to far corner to go over stile. The path leads on to a lane. Walk along the cobbled lane to Brinscall.

Brinscall

Brinscall is first mentioned in 1200, then named Brendescoles, meaning 'the burnt huts'. Why the huts were burnt is lost to the record of pre-history; all we can say is that it must have once been a Scandinavian settlement some-time before the Norman Conquest. During the 10th century, Norse farmers settled on the marginal lands on the edges of the old shires of Leyland, Blackburn and Amounderness.

Today the once thriving weaving village is fading back into the surround-ing rural landscape. Little moves apart from strollers around the water's edge, the railway has been and gone and only the ducks remain to break the peace of a Sunday afternoon.

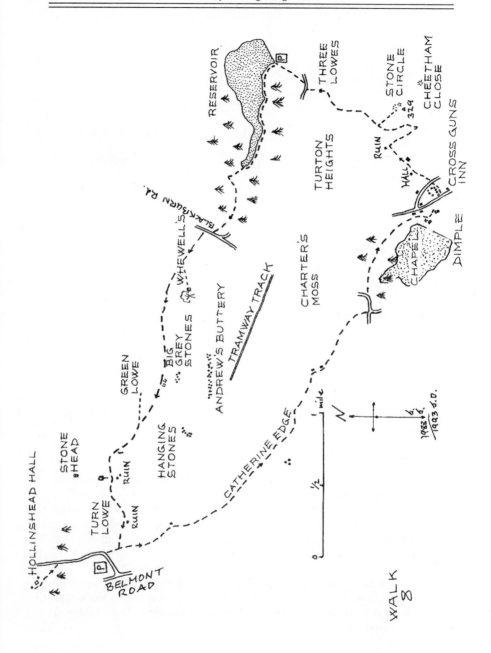

Walk 8

THE STONES OF
ICE AND MEN

12 miles, 6 hours

MAP: *O.S. SD 61/71 PATHFINDER Series*

LUNCH: *Cross Guns, Dimple*

START: *Tockholes Road parking area (SD 192 665)*

For those with a love of wild moorland, broken only by sheets of clear blue waters, this walk offers many pleasures. The retreating ice has carved massive hillside formations like the hanging stones and fortress-type structures we see on Andrew's Buttery and above Green Lowe.

Man too has left his mark with stones in the form of circles and ring-bank cairns established in the Bronze Age, and the gritstone farmsteads of a later age that now lie derelict across the moors. This walk explores man's life and environment on these windswept hilltops from early times to the present day, taking in a wide variety of places of interest.

For lunch we recommend the Cross Guns Inn at Dimple, where good food is served at very reasonable prices. But don't feast too well for you've Turton Heights in front of you.

Tockholes Road Parking Area to Dimple Chapel

Walk up to the corner to pass over stile by gate on the right. The track leads on, past the house, over the moors to meet with the roadway above Delph Reservoir. Left and walk down the road to pass through a gate on the right. The path leads us down to pass over a footbridge, then on up to the right to enter a wood via stile by gate. Pass through the wood to leave by stile. The path leads us over the field to enter a cobbled terraced street via stile. Walk along the street to directly enter a pathway that leads down to the churchyard gates.

Charters Moss

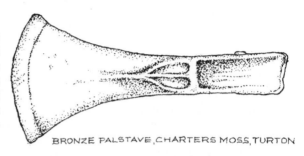

Peat digging on the moss has revealed many Bronze Age finds, the best examples being a perforated stone hammer and a bronze palstave (pictured right).

BRONZE PALSTAVE, CHARTERS MOSS, TURTON

Other finds in the area have been a looped socketed spearhead with part of its original wooden shaft, a more developed palstave with improved hafting, and a loop-headed spearhead of bronze. All the items found display a high standard of workmanship in their manufacture suggesting a well-developed and prosperous community living in the area.

Walmsley Chapel, Dimple

The Walmsley Unitarian Chapel stands near the Walmsley School of 1851 in an isolated spot away from the busy main road. The Chapel was built in 1713 and must be one of the oldest of its type in the District — notice the datestone below the gable bellcote.

UNITARIAN CHAPEL DIMPLE

The front is altered from the original. The sides, however, are original having two tiers of small three-light mullioned windows. Inside are box pews and a pulpit from the early 18th century. The chapel originally stood on the old Egerton Road, now the back road. Its site can still be seen today on the edge of the new estate at the top of the brookside path we take past the estate, on the right.

On our way to the Cross Guns we shall pass Howarths Farm, and a close inspection will reveal some of its 17th century features.

Unitarian Chapel to Cross Guns Inn

Come out of the churchyard and walk down the lane on the right for a few yards to pass over stile on left. Cross the field to pass over stile by barn and on past side of farm to follow farm lane to the main road. Turn right and walk down to the pub.

Cross Guns to Dimple Hall

Walk back up the road to turn right into grassed trackway on edge of new estate. Follow path up to the roadway. Cross the road to go over stile opposite. Walk up the field on a left diagonal to gateway and on to Dimple Hall.

Dimple Hall

Dimple Hall is a mid-Victorian house done in the Gothic revival style. The datestone bears the initials P.H.A. with a date of 1855. With its open gallery and cross windows, it creates a most pleasing picture to the eye.

Dimple Hall to Stone Circles

Walk up the lane to enter High Lands yard. Pass over stile opposite and follow path up to the trees. Walk to the right to gate-stile in wall (DO NOT PASS OVER). Follow wallside path up and on past the corner, over the moor to pass through old narrow gateway in wall. Walk on to the 'white pole', right and follow the path along the old field boundary to the Trig. Point via stile.

Cheetham Close Stone Circle Complex

Situated on the bleak moorland plateau of Cheetham Close, above Turton, stands an Early Bronze Age village and burial complex. It consists of a stone circle with at least two outliers, two ring-bank cairns and two small cairns of unknown structure.

The stone circle is now in a ruinous condition. Ten stones originally formed the circle and though many have been broken and displaced, it is still possible to discern the original settings. At a distance of 45 feet south-west from the circle stands a solitary stone 19 inches high, and south-west at a distance of 102 feet another can be found.

The ring-bank cairn is located just south of the stone circle, on slightly higher ground. Its circular shape is defined by a low, annular rubble and earth bank. When excavated in 1893 it was claimed that the bank was faced both externally and internally by large gritstone slabs set contiguously in a kerb. A possible entrance exists in the north-east quadrant, where a gap about 1m wide is flanked by much thicker sections of bank.

In the centre is a low cairn, not clearly defined on the west, and partially destroyed by illicit excavators. A small satellite cairn, 2m in diameter, lies in the north-east quadrant. Two other small cairns lie to the north-east and to the south-east of the stone circle and ring-bank cairn respectively.

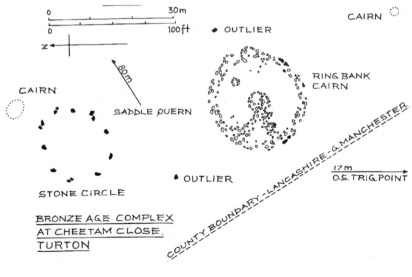

STONE CIRCLE, TURTON

Another ring-bank cairn has been located 700m south-east of the triangulation pillar. It is partially overlain by a stone wall and in a ruinous condition, yet sections of the massive rubble kerb can be distinguished, and a large earthfast boulder near the centre may be an integral feature.

In 1954 a Bronze Age saddle quern was found 80m north-east of the stone circle. These were used for grinding cereal grains into a rough flour. Three barbed-and-tanged arrowheads were also found. For most of the above information, we are indebted to M. Fletcher for his survey work on the above sites.

SADDLE QUERN.

Much controversy exists as to the function of such stone circles and cairns, with theories ranging from ancient temples to agrarian calendars. However, it is now thought that these complexes represent contemporary sites for ritual and burial respectively, yet even the latter mode of thinking can only explain a part of their role and function. A more interdisciplinary approach is needed to fully understand their true nature, and our starting point must be the first permanent settlement in such places as Turton Heights.

Before the forest clearance down to the valley floors during the Middle to Later Bronze Ages, which brought soil erosion and impoverishment to the Pennine uplands, such highland sites would have been viable economic settlement units. On looking north from the cairn, it is not hard to imagine cultivated fields stretching across the plateau — the finding of the saddle quern testifies to such activity in close proximity to the circles.

What then of the circles themselves? First let us look at the structure referred to as a ring-bank cairn. When excavated, the majority of such sites yield many urn-burial cremations. This fact has led many archaeologists to interpret the site solely in terms of a burial complex. If such well-built structures were built for the dead then what fine structures the community's dwellings must have been, and indeed where are they today?

For the answer one must re-examine the ring-bank cairn in wider terms. The cairn itself is simultaneously a place of the living and of the dead. It could well be what remains of a communal living hut with ancestral remains interred beneath the place that was most central to their lives — a well revetted stone-walled building with a turf roof supported by timbers. In the centre of the hut would be a hearth and chimney stack.

We now turn our attention to the stone circle. Again this could be the foundations of a building but this is doubtful. A more likely explanation is that it is a statement of the establishment of territorial rights over an area by an economic and social group. A small group of persons squatting on a highland plateau gives no sign to others of permanence — they can easily be displaced.

But the erection of a monument that has consumed some communal economic effort implies to others a permanence of settlement, a physical statement — 'We are here, this is ours'. Later such places would gain a symbolic, religious and secular significance — a place of social and economic exchange. The site at Cheetham Close may have been a regional centre with satellite communities on the surrounding hilltops of Winter Hill, Darwen Moor and Anglezarke Moor. As each year goes by, more and more sites come to light in these areas.

Stone Circles to Turton & Entwistle Reservoir Car Park

Walk back to the white pole and turn right to follow old field boundary to its corner, overlooking Three Lowes. Cross the field on a left diagonal down to go over corner stile near ruin. Follow well-defined pathway on, between the Lowes, to go over fence stile. Follow fence down to roadway. Turn right and walk down the road to go left over stile at footpath sign. Walk down to go over stile and on down to pass through green gate to walk down to the car park.

Car Park to Whewell's Ruin

The waterside path leads us to the wooded start of the waters and on up to an old quarry face and on up, obtaining magnificent views over the waters and Holcombe Moor, to meet with the main Blackburn Road. Right, and walk along the road for about 100 yards to enter pathway on left. Walk up the path to a level with the lone tree over on the left. Walk over to the tree and ruin of Whewell's.

Whewell's

Whewell's is just another hillside ruin, remarkable only for its large beehive cellars. Above Whewell's are the moors of Turton and Longworth on whose tops are to be found several stone outcrops. The Hanging Stones, the Big Grey Stones and Andrews Buttery are huge arrangements of boulders, deeply scarred by the retreating ice of the glacier that deposited them there.

The Darwen Moor Head SD 675195

This large and grotesque stone head was found some years ago near the old mine shafts on Darwen Moor. Today it can be found on display in the Ribchester Roman Museum along with other so-called 'Celtic Heads'. Given the style of workmanship I doubt whether this head belongs to any of the early historical periods, its origins must be sought in the Victorian period. But I may be wrong.

THE DARWEN
MOOR HEAD

The survival of some of the true Celtic stone heads is linked mainly to the ancient cult of the severed head. To the Celts, in the head rested everything that made men what they are — it was the seat of the Celtic equivalent of the soul. Celtic warriors were head-hunters who kept the heads of their foes as trophies and Brigantian forts were adorned with human heads. Stone heads, not unlike the one found upon Darwen Moor, appear to have represented Celtic deities such as Maponus, the northern god.

Stone heads have been invested with special properties in local superstitions, right up to the present day. Relics of an older paganism survive in many forms in modern Christianity; green men, imps, bearded ogres and whores adorn many of our local churches. The power of pagan superstition is long-lived and not easily set aside by reason.

Whewell's to Parking Area on Tockholes Road

Return back to the pathway and follow it up to pass over fence-stile. The path leads us past the spoil heaps and takes us over the moor to meet with a well-defined path. This in turn leads us up to a 'pole' and on to meet with a footpath sign (Peak District & Northern Counties Footpath Preservation Society. Erected by the Ramblers Association, 24 April 1960). The Celtic Head was found to the north of this footpath sign. The Belmont path leads us down to a lower trackway and back to the parking area.

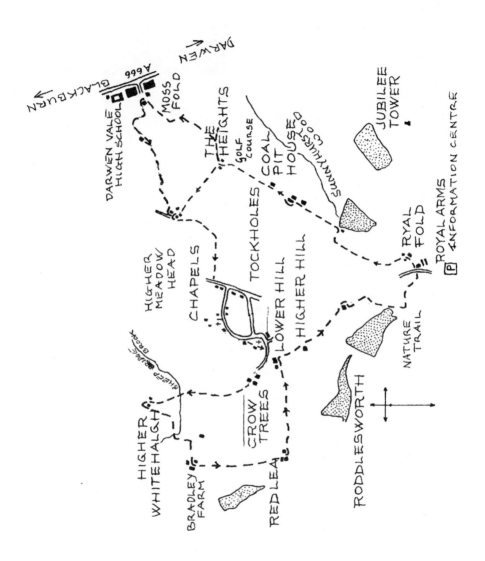

Walk 9

LIVESEY-CUM-TOCKHOLES

Ryal Fold, The Moss, Tockholes,
Whitehalgh & Roddlesworth

9 miles, 5 hours

MAP: *O.S. SD 62/72 PATHFINDER Series*

LUNCH: *Royal Arms, Tockholes or Rock Inn, Tockholes*

START: *Information Centre Car Park, Royal Arms*
            (SD 665 215)

Set in hidden rural splendour on Blackburn's south-western boundary can be found the ancient manor of Livesey-cum-Tockholes. Rationalised farming hardly seems to have affected the area. Old trackways of an earlier coaching age can still be discerned and many old 16th-century houses and farmsteads still stand proud, all recalling the charm of a former rural age.

Tockholes is and always will be an enigma, with its stories of treacle mines, of the flight of Prince Rupert against Cromwell's might, of ancient stones and coaching roads. Nothing is recorded but much is recalled by local families who claim descent from Toca, a legendary figure whose story is lost to the mists of time.

The walk takes in ten sites of historical and architectural interest through a landscape which will remain in one's mind forever.

The Royal Arms

The Royal Arms makes a good starting point, with easy access to car parking and bus stops, along with genial hospitality, good ale and very reasonably priced lunches served in most rustic surroundings, all add up to a day out to remember.

The hillsides to the south-east of the pub where once the medieval common pastureland for the village of Tockholes and upon Cartridge Hill can be found a number of disused coal mines. Eccles Shorrock, a Darwen cotton manufacturer and Lord of the Manor of Tockholes in the 19th century, owned the mines and used the coal to fuel Hollinshead Mill that once stood alongside the Royal Arms. The mill workers lived in the rows of terraced cottages beyond.

The Roddlesworth Information Centre provides details on the West Pennine Moors Access Areas, Nature Trail leaflets and information on conservation work in the area.

Royal Arms to Ryal Fold

Walk down the lane at the side of the pub to enter Ryal Fold.

Ryal Fold

Ryal Fold is a small group of farmhouses and cottages which date from the 17th century, situated at the foot of Tockholes Moor and Earndale Reservoir. As is recorded on the date-stone, the yeoman farmhouse pictured here was built for John and Elizabeth Walmsley in 1676. The owners of an earlier house on the site were the Marsdens. Hugh Marsden of Ryal is recorded as having paid the King's Subsidy Tax in 1523, and William Marsden was a governor of Blackburn Grammar School in 1634.

The house has an interesting design with a fine gabled porch. Here we see a round-headed main entrance doorway, above which the three-light mullioned window has round-headed lights, and above this is a single round-headed window set in the gable. An incongruous lean-to has been built on to the front, which ought to be removed if the house is to be returned to its ancient splendour. The barn standing opposite the house is one of the finest examples of watershot stone walling in this part of Lancashire. Indeed, so well is the stone cut that one could almost walk up the wall sides.

Another house at Ryal has been recently modernised to a large degree, but still shows some of the early 17th-century mullioned windows with hood-moulds.

Ryal Fold to Moss Fold

Pass through the farmyard gate and walk down the old farm lane to pass through next gate. Follow field boundary to the right, down and up to pass through wall gate. Walk down to the right to the head of the reservoir to pass over cattle-grid on left. Walk up the lane to Berry's Tenement Farm (built into the wall by the gate is an old millstone with the inscription: 'IN MEMORY OF ABELLA WIFE OF DUXBURY').

Pass through gateway and walk around the new shed to go over stile by gate on to golf course. Walk directly on to follow trackway over the golf course to enter pathway at the Height at 'Hole 11'. Walk on and down the farm lane to above the Club House to go over stile by gate on left. Walk down the field to pass over fence-stile on right. Cross the playing field to the rear of the housing estate. Take the path down to the left, through stile and on across the field to go through gate down on the right. The old lane leads to Moss Fold (to the left).

THE MOSS

The Moss

Lower Moss is a grade III listed building, sadly going to rack and ruin at this moment in time. How unfortunate that such a fine 17th-century farmhouse has today been relegated to the position of a mere junk store.

The front of the house displays a flat-fronted porch with a wide off-set doorway and a tiny two-light mullioned window below the roof-line. All its ancient mullioned windows remain, though some are now bricked-up. The gable chimney is worthy of note, being one of the few examples in the area of original Jacobean moulded-edge type. To the rear is a gable projecting from the centre. The upper floor of the rear displays mullioned windows.

It would be to Darwen's credit if this building could be restored, as Moss Fold, fronted by its running waters, could be a very attractive spot indeed.

Above Moss Fold stands the whitewashed farmstead of Greenlands. Close inspection of this hillside dwelling will reveal traces of its ancient mullioned windows. Look at the two odd windows to the left of the porch, and again high in the side gable.

Moss Fold to Higher Meadow Head Farm

Pass through the farmyard and take the farm lane around the school playing field up to Greenlands Farm. Continue on up the green lane to enter field and pass over wallside stile up on the right. Walk along the wallside to pass over fence-stile and follow field boundary to the right, and up to pass over stile by gate. Walk on to go over stile on right and walk past the edge of garden on to lane. Walk up to Higher Meadow Head.

Higher Meadow Head Farm, Tockholes

The farmstead comprises a ruined 17th-century farmhouse, barn and shippon of the 19th century and a 20th-century farmhouse.

The shippon, which appears at one time to have doubled as a hen house, has a flight of 'fox' steps leading to the first floor; these are situated in the outside gable.

The farmer is of the opinion that the barn used to be an inn standing on the route that coaches took travelling between Belthorn, Tockholes and Feniscowles in the 18th and 19th centuries. It seems unlikely that the present building served this purpose as it appeared to be a late-Victorian purpose built barn. However, the first O.S. map of the 1840s does not appear to show this building but a smaller one in a slightly different position, so this one could conceivably have been the inn.

The ruined farmhouse has unfortunately had its date-stone stolen but the farmer recollects it as being 1688, the same as Earcroft Barn.

The building is constructed of stone and appears to have been built in two stages and styles. The only complete wall still standing is the west-facing gable which has at ground floor level a small round-headed window of a 17th-century date.

Higher Meadow Head to St. Stephens, Chapels

Take the green lane opposite the double garage, across a track at an old farm entrance, directly on to meet with a farm lane that leads to the road. Pass The Rock Inn (Roger & Ann Roscorn 1791) to go down Rock Lane to the churchyard.

St Stephen's School and Church

The church was built between 1831-33, and today only the front of the south porch has been preserved. It now leads to a modern church building of 1965. Propped up against the church walls are a number of decorated stone slabs bearing heraldic designs.

The prized possession of the churchyard is the ancient Toches Stone. Its plinth, a retooled cheese-press weight, is inscribed and informs us:

'The upper portion of this monument is supposed to be a remnant of the old Parish Preaching Cross probably dating from 984. The lower portion is probably a part of the ancient Toches Stone from which the parish took its name'.

The place-name of Tockholes is Old English and means 'Tocca's Valley', Tocca being an old Saxon personal name going back to the 8th century.

TOCHES STONE

St Stephen's School was erected in 1854 upon the glebe land by voluntary subscription, aided by a grant from the National Society in London. The open-air pulpit, built of window mullions, is of around 1900-10, replacing an earlier wooden one from Mellor Church.

All in all St Stephen's churchyard presents the strangest variety of church buildings and sculpture I have ever seen, all adding to the mystery and folklore of Tockholes.

CHAPELS FARM, TOCHOLES

Chapels Farm and Old Well

Standing on the opposite side to the church is the 17th-century building of Chapels Farm.

A little way up the lane, to the east of the church, stands a castellated roadside well. An inscribed stone inside the well's round-headed arch informs us that 'The Norman arch over this well was removed from Gerstane Hall, Tockholes — Gerstane or Garstang Hall stood before its demolition near to the Royal Arms Hotel at Ryal — and placed here in 1910 by the Rev. A. T. Cornfield'. Beneath the inscription is an heraldic shield with the Latin scroll 'Serva Fidem'.

Even in my youth the community at Tockholes was still served by local wells for the supply of water. One I remember well stands opposite the Bull Inn, but with all the chemicals used on the land today I could not recommend its usage. Near to the Bull Inn there once stood an ancient cross, said to have been mutilated by Roundhead soldiers during the Civil Wars.

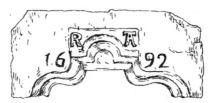

On the same roadway as Chapels Well can be found an old doorhead, now used as a wall gate lintel, with a date 1692 and the initials R.A., displayed within an ogee framework.

DOORHEAD, TOCKHOLES

Chapels to Higher & Lower Crow Trees

Continue along the lane to go through footpath gate by Lodge Farm. After passing through the next gate cross the field to go over wall-stile into farmyard. Pass through and up to the lane. Right, and walk on to Higher then Lower Crow Trees.

Higher and Lower Crow Trees

Higher Crow Trees is a much altered 17th-century house. Remains of the old mullioned windows and hood moulds can still be made out. To the right of the lean-to doorway is a small round-headed window above which are the initials I.M., being those of John Marsden of Tockholes.

The field opposite Crow Trees is known as Kill or Pit Field. It was here in 1833 that thirty eight horses' heads, various bones and a number of cannon balls were dug up. The finds were said to be the relics of a battle fought nearby in around 1642 during the Civil War. Once again we find a claim for the Battle of Darwen Moor, though in this part of Tockholes they claim that the dead are buried in the old Tockholes churchyard, which was demolished in 1832.

Lower Crow Trees is another 17th-century house, the mullioned windows with drip-mouldings presenting a fine frontage. Above a doorway on the barn opposite is an inscribed stone bearing the initials W.M., and the date 1671. The house is thought to be an old coaching house and stables. In fact Lower Crow Trees stands on the fork of two ancient trackways. Both are metalled:

one crosses the fields to Red Lea Farm and the other we shall walk along to Higher Whitehalgh where you will notice gateposts in the stream by the footbridge. The road is said to be the old coaching road between Bolton and Clitheroe.

Lower Crow Trees to Higher Whitehalgh

Pass over stile by bottom field gate and walk on to pass over fence-stile on right. Walk on to walk by the side of the Motor Cross track and as the track enters the lower wood and veers off to the left simply walk down the wooded bank to find and cross a footbridge. Walk up the bank to pass over wall-stile and on up the field to pass over stile by gate at Higher Whitehalgh.

Higher Whitehalgh

The ivy all but hides the fine 17th-century farmhouse of Higher Whitehalgh. The asymmetrical north-west frontage holds a fine selection of mullioned windows. The off-centre gabled porch has a datestone above the upper floor window, 1616, with the initials of the builder Thomas Livesey, along with the initials G.MR.S.

HIGHER WHITEHALGH

Whitehalgh was given in the time of Edward I, by William, son of Henry de Livesey, to Richard his brother for a yearly rent of two shillings. During the reign of Edward II a William Livesey adopted Whitehalgh as his surname. The Livesey family claim to have lived on the site since they first built a dwelling here in 940 and, given that they are one of the oldest families in Lancashire, this may well be so.

Many folk tales have grown up around Whitehalgh. The most noted is that Oliver Cromwell is said to have stayed three nights in the house, during which time he and his men fought the Battle of Darwen Moor. The story goes that the three hundred men who died in the battle are buried in the sandy field facing the house. Cromwell is supposed to have spoken words over them from an open pulpit built into the gable-end of the house. Locals point to the hood-mouldings set in the gable as being all that remains of the pulpit.

The Witches of Whitehalgh

It was during the reign of the Calvinist James I that Thomas Livesey, of the family Livesey, lords of Livesey-cum-Tock-holes, built his fine yeoman farmhouse on the hundred acre portion of Livesey known as Higher Whitehalgh.

In ancient times this had been the site of the great Manoral Hall of Livesey, the first such edifice being erected in 940 AD as an expression of land right and overlordship against the expansion of the Hiberno-Norse Vikings under their chief Gunnolf, who had colonised much of the surrounding districts between Leylandshire and Blackburnshire. During the 12th century the Manoral seat was moved to an eminence overlooking their corn-mill enterprise at Tongue in Pleasington. Their Hall was to remain upon this new site till the demolition of the final building there in the 1960s.

The early 17th century was a troubled time for Lancashire Catholics, and an even worse time for the many Irish immigrants who sought and gained work as farmhands in the sympathetic Catholic North Lancashire. With the failure of the Catholic zealot's Gunpowder Plot in advent of their non-success to secure a relaxation of the laws against Catholicism on James's succession, fear of Catholicism was raised to a fever pitch, the hysteria was to spread to every corner of rural England. Even the fervently Catholic redoubt of North Lancashire was forced inwards to cloak and shroud itself in a mantle of secrecy against the prevailings winds of retribution.

Hoghton Tower, the largest and most important gentleman's house in the lower Darwen Valley, would have been the natural key centre for the survival of the Catholic Mass but for the misfortunes of its owners. Sir Thomas de Hoghton fled the country in 1568 in order to escape persecution, and died in exile. His son, a priest, died in prison. The direct line failed, and in 1589 the infant heir, Richard, was placed in Protestant hands to be brought up. It was this Richard, 'Honest Dick' as he was known at court, who entertained James I in 1617, an occasion that led to the knighting of 'Sir Loin' of beef.

With the decline of Hoghton Tower as a Catholic stronghold the burden of responsibility for survival of the Faith and Mass fell upon the shoulders of lesser yeoman stock. Therefore when Thomas Livesey built his fine new house in 1616 he incorporated into its design several unusual features. Large cavities were built into the stone walls at different levels, interconnected by means of hidden stairwells. Here then is one of many examples to be found in Lancashire of Priest Hiding Holes. In later years the secret passages at Whitehalgh were to be put to a stranger use.

During the 17th Lancashire was host to many Irish immigrants, who sought refuge from the English Protestant conquest and colonisation of Ireland. The newcomers, it is said, not only brought their families but also the tiny folk known as leprechauns. From what I am told these little peoples have visited Lancashire since ancient times providing such services, given their close understanding of Nature, as breeders and healers of animals. Through their efforts Lancashire and those areas west of the Pennines were able to breed such fine cattle and horse.

The local Catholics saw this new influx of tiny folk as a hindrance compounding their already heavy burden of troubles, adding strength to those who saw their practices as superstitious and the work of the Devil.

So the Irish leprechauns found oppresser and oppressed to be their foe; very few valued their veterinary services, the Livesey's of Whitehalgh being of the few.

From the safety of former priestly hides the leprechauns went forth to the aid of those who knew well of their powers, down the centuries their methods tried and trusted. In woodland their presence was never seen, but on open ground, when about their travels, they were often seen to run swiftly for the safety of the far dell or glade. Even today their number still thrive and many attest to have seen their fleeting shadows and heard the sound of their brisk footfall in the wooded ravines that surround Whitehalgh. And on a cool summer's evening their singing, carried on the balmy air, can be heard as they feast and make merry by the waterfall in Sheep Bridge Brook.

On the eve of the old festivals, and on a Hunter's Moon, their gatherings at Whitehalgh are a sight to be witnessed only by the trusted and honest few. On such nights the farmhouse garden hosts a carnival of the woodland neverworld folk, the elders and wise ones holding court upon the 'witches stone'; an old cheese-press base marked with an encircled cross between hidden letters 'H' and 'T' — "Honest and truthful for all to see, then trusted thee be."

Here the old ways are recalled to be passed on to future generations so good work may continue. If an infant has borne to the folk the small baptismal font is brought forth from the rear of the house and the duties performed to the custom of ancient lore. As the night turns to daybreak and us larger human forms stir in our beds, the gathering fades to leave only the sound of the cock to herald a new day, and a farmstead wakes to cloggs on cobbled stone, cows come for milking, the farm day begins.

The respectful visitor to Whitehalgh, if she or he worthy, may have the Witches Stone and the baptismal font shown to them. And for those who scorn such things, then they best be on their way lest the sky fall in on them.

Other Priest Holes in Livesey-cum-Tockholes

At RED LEA a hiding hole is built into the side of the large inglenook fireplace, being part of an older house of the late 16th century built by the Hoghton family. The present house is dated 1674 with the initials of Richard and Elizabeth (Hoghton) Aspden.

Below the stairwell leading to medieval latrine at HIGHER HILL can be found a hidden recess, allowing enough space to secrete oneself for a short time. LOWER HILL MANOR HOUSE is said to have been a place where mass was held in secret, a lamp being lit and placed in a rear window as a signal to local Catholics of the priest's presence.

Higher Whitehalgh to Red Lea

Pass through the farmyard on to lane, then down the lane on the left that crosses the brook and leads up to a junction. Right, and walk on to enter Bradley farmyard. The track now goes between the barns and crosses the fields to Red Lea. Walk to the front of the main house.

Red Lea

Red Lea is an old hamlet which stands above the River Roddlesworth, secluded by woods on its western side and which contains a small number of 17th century buildings. The best preserved of these is Red Lea Farm, a solid stone-built house with many interesting features. Mullioned windows complete with hood-moulds add charm to the asymmetrical frontage. The gabled storeyed porch has an off-centre doorway, and above the drip-moulding a framed date tablet is set in the stonework. It bears the initials of Richard and Elizabeth (or Ellen) Aspden and the date 1674.

RED LEA

A branch of the Hoghton family of Hoghton Tower lived at Red Lea during the 16th and 17th centuries. William Hoghton, second son of Richard Hoghton of Tockholes, appears in the records in 1602, and died at Red Lea in 1623. When Elizabeth Hoghton married Richard Aspden the house of Red Lea was rebuilt for them. Inside is a large Inglenook fireplace and a priest's hiding hole. Richard was a trustee in a deed of gift to Tockholes Chapel in 1670 and one Thomas Aspden of Red Lea was a trustee of the Nonconformist Meeting House in 1735.

Red Lea to Lower Hill Manor House

Walk past the front of Red Lea Farm to rear of house to go over stile. Follow old trackway to go over slab-bridge and stile on the left, follow fence to go over next stile. Walk up the field on a left diagonal to old marl pit. Walk around on right of pit and on to old gate posts. Follow trackway to Manor House.

Lower Hill Manor House

The large 17th-century building of Lower Hill, formerly known as the Manor House, has now been converted into four cottages. Along with the odd sized gables and built-on extensions the house presents a very distorted frontage. Happily all the original features remain and with a little thought and co-operation Lower Hill could easily be restored to its former glory.

One feature that has been restored by one of the tenants is a small window overlooking the valley. In those dark days when the Roman Faith was outlawed, a lamp would be lit and placed in the window as a signal to the local populace that a priest was about to hold a secret Mass. Adam Richardson is recorded to have lived at Lower Hill in 1735. It was his second son Ralph who built the Silk Hall in 1764.

Manor House to Higher Hill

From the front of Manor House walk up to go through gated wall stile. Follow wall up to Higher Hill.

Higher Hill

Higher Hill is by far the most outstanding house in Tockholes.

It was built by Ralph Walmsley in 1612. His initials and the date are inscribed upon a small round-headed window on the north face of the house. Ralph died on the 22nd November, 1665, at the age of 100 years, and is buried in Blackburn churchyard (now the Cathedral grounds).

Roger de Walmerslegh was living in an earlier house on the site in 1334, and from a branch of his family descended the notable families of Walmsley of Showley Hall and Walmsley of Dunkenhalgh.

The gabled porch is a very solid looking structure. Above the doorway, where one would usually expect to find the stone date tablet, is a carved head surrounded by mouldings. Above is a three-light mullioned window with hood mouldings above. Set in the gable is a round-headed niche, perhaps for holding a figure. Another niche can be found on the ground floor of the south-wing gable-end. Below the valley of the south wall is a medieval latrine set on corbels; inside, the wooden seat still exists — so look up with care.

To the south of Higher Hill lies the wooded valley of the River Roddlesworth. A nature trail has been made through the wood and starts at the Royal Arms Hotel; details and a map can be found on a notice board near the pub.

Higher Hill to the Royal Arms

Pass over stile by gate and walk over to footpath sign. Take the higher path over the fields to go over stile by gate at trees. Walk down the drive to front of cottage. Walk over to the left (rather overgrown at moment) to pass over wall-stile. Walk directly over the field to enter wood via stile. The path leads down to above the reservoir where we take any path to the left till we meet a well made path that will lead us up to the Royal Arms.

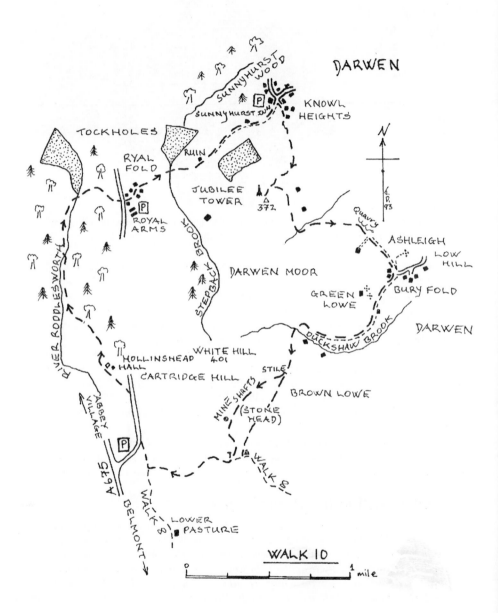

WALK 10

TOCKHOLES
RYAL FOLD
ROYAL ARMS
SUNNYHURST WOOD
DARWEN
SUNNYHURST INN
KNOWL HEIGHTS
RUIN
JUBILEE TOWER
△ 372
N
6. D. 93
Quavy
ASHLEIGH
LOW HILL
BURY FOLD
DARWEN MOOR
STEPBACK BROOK
GREEN LOWE
DUCKSHAW BROOK
DARWEN
RIVER RODDLESWORTH
HOLLINSHEAD HALL
WHITE HILL 401
CARTRIDGE HILL
STILE
BROWN LOWE
MINESHAFTS
(STONE HEAD)
WALK 8
ABBEY VILLAGE
A 675
WALK 8
BELMONT →
LOWER PASTURE

WALK 10

0   1 mile

Walk 10

MOORLAND TOWER
TO
WOODLAND HALL

Darwen Moor, Hollinshead Hall ramble

8 miles, 4 hours

MAP: *O.S. SD 62/72 & 61/71 PATHFINDER Series*

LUNCH: *Royal Arms, Tockholes, or Sunnyhurst Inn*

START: *Information centre Car Park, Royal Arms*
                  or Sunnyhurst Wood top car park

On this walk we climb above Tockholes to view the ancient 'oak valley' from the hilltop vantage point Jubilee Tower. Darwen is a typical solid stone-hewn northern town, clearly an expression of the industrial age that spawned such places.

The image it presents is that of the world of the late 19th century, but if one looks more closely, its former rural past can be discerned.

Today, we wander through that former time before King Cotton ruled and explore the more pastoral aspects of the district.

Royal Arms to Jubilee Tower

Walk down the farm lane by the side of the pub to go through a small gate (footpath marker) on the right at the entry to Ryal Fold Farm. The way takes us over a stile and down the right edge of the field to pass through a small gate.

The path leads up to pass through an old iron revolving gate to meet an access road that takes us past the Water Works house to the Sunnyhurst Inn. Opposite the pub a track leads us up to the Jubilee Tower.

Jubilee Tower

The eighty-six foot high Darwen Tower, as it is locally known, was erected in 1898 to mark the Jubilee of Queen Victoria. The tower dominates the skyline for miles around and provides a vantage point from which the surrounding countryside can be viewed.

The edifice stands on the summit of Beacon Hill, named after the ancient signal beacon that once stood here. The fire-beacon would be lit to commemorate an event or Saint's day and sometimes to signal approaching danger or as a rallying sign for the local militia.

On a good clear day the peaks of the Yorkshire Dales can be made out beyond the bulk of Pendle, Ingleborough and Pen-y-ghent being dominant. Beyond the Forest of Bowland, to the north west, the mountains of the Lake District provide a rugged skyline. And if we are very lucky we may just be able to pick out the Isle of Man out in the Irish Sea.

Jubilee Tower to Bury Fold

Walk down the eastern path to go right at the cross-paths. Walk on then down to the left, through gate and on down to pass through next gate. From here pass through fence-stile up on the right. Walk on over the rough and follow the path round to the left to pass through stile. Walk along the fence-line to pass through double stile. Walk directly on and down the farm road to meet with the Bury Fold road. Left and walk down some 100 yards to enter Bury Fold on the right (Low Hill House is further down the road on the right).

Bury Fold

Bury Fold takes its name from the Burry family who lived here between 1520 and 1850. William Berre was assessed for lands in Darwen in 1523. In 1672, another William Berry, a Nonconformist, had the house at Bury Fold licensed as a preaching place. The Nonconformist doctrine spread many strong roots in the Darwen area among a people who have always had an independent attitude towards life.

The farmhouse at Bury Fold is now divided into three dwellings, yet this does not detract from it being a very imposing structure, retaining its own ancient individual character, this being mainly due to the high standard of restoration carried out by its owners.

The house's dominant feature is its massive central multi-storey porch with projecting upper-walls. The offset doorway displays a deeply cut ogee door head above which is a datestone of 1673 with the arms of the Burry family. The first-floor porch window has an ogee head and hood mould, and above this is a two-light round-headed mullioned window. All in all a very pleasing edifice.

Bronze Age Ring-Bank Burial Mound, Ashleigh Street, Darwen

No physical evidence remains of Darwen's only known barrow, it having been destroyed during October 1864 as excavations were being made for the foundations of Ashleigh House, which incidentally was itself demolished during 1986.

Contemporary reports about its excavation state that it was of circular form about 30 yards in diameter, being formed on a naze or promontory of an undulating plateau overlooking the Darwen Valley. Its height was said to vary from 10 to 12 feet on the east side and between 2 or 3 feet on the west, the centre being about 6 feet in diameter and consisting of a slight hollow.

Ten internments appear to have been made, one being just a heap of burnt bones, the others, having been enclosed in urns, the majority of which are badly broken, consisted of ashes and fragments of bone together with unrecognisable pieces of bronze. Two urns also contained 'incense cups' and another a 7½" bronze knife or dagger.

The design of the urns is similar to those from the Middle Bronze Age (1200/1500 B.C.). All but two of the urns were found within an area 21 ft by 14 ft, whilst one was 40 feet away. They were, with one exception, placed in the earth with the orifice pointing upwards and were covered with slabs, the depth at which they were found varying from 1 to 2 feet.

Many superstitions were attached to the barrow and its destruction in the 1860s, with the country people speaking of the place being haunted by 'boggarts' and children having been known to take off their clogs or shoes and walk past it barefoot in the night time.

An excavation which took place in 1986 found only evidence of the original lie of the land, the naze apparently having been levelled during the construction of the house.

For over ninety years the Whitehall Urns have been on display in the Reference Library at Darwen — safe, but still accessible to the public. Some time ago the urns were taken by the County Archaeologist, Ben Edwards, to be restored by Lancashire Museums Service. This work has now been done and the urns are due to be returned to the Reference Library at Darwen.

Two other possible Bronze Age sites

Two mounds stand to the east across from Green Lowe Farm. The meadow in which they stand is used for grazing and the mounds have not been ex-cavated. The name 'lowe' is often an indication of a burial mound, and the mounds at Green Lowe do not appear to be natural formations. Given the field evidence, a survey of this possible site is called for.

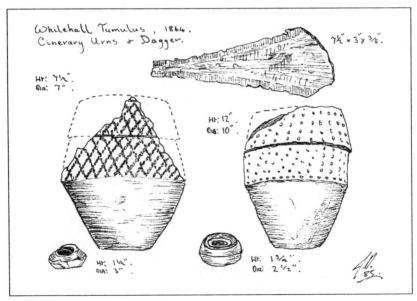

Low Hill House

Low Hill House was built in 1812 and was, until 1817, the home of Samuel Crompton, inventor of the spinning mule. The east and west wings were added later by Eccles Shorrock. Crompton's spinning mule is on display in Lewis Textile Museum, Blackburn.

Bury Fold to Hollinshead Hall

Return back up the road and follow it up (Green Lowe Farm can be seen over on the right and the mounds can be viewed in the field between) till you come to a pair of ornamental gates. Pass through the side and walk along the driveway a short way to take a track up to the right, and after passing through a gate walk on up to go left at junction of tracks.

Continue on over the moor to pass over stile. From here the direct path leads to a stone cairn, then to the right to meet a footpath sign — but this way can be very boggy and I suggest you take the slight path to the right that leads past the old mine pits to the footpath sign.

From the sign post, the path leads down to meet a good track that leads us to the Tockholes road. Walk up the road and over the brow to pass through gate on left at wood. Walk down the path to the ruins of Hollinshead Hall.

Hollinshead Hall

In the early 1200s the manor of Tockholes, in the township of Livesey was in the possession of a branch of the de Pleasington family who took the local name as their surname.

The de Tocholes were later followed by the Radcliffes of Ordall who had their manor house on the site of Lower Hill cottages. They held the manor until 1641 when it was sold.

Part of the manor, the Hollinshead, was purchased by Edward Warren who built a large yeoman farmhouse there. In 1666 he was assessed for tax on eight hearths in his properties there.

Some time after 1761 the house and lands were sold to John Hollinshead. Being in a ruinous condition at that time, the house was for the most part demolished and rebuilt in 1776. The Well House was also built at this time, replacing the old farm well.

Upon the death of John Hollinshead, the estate descended to his cousin William Brock, who assumed the additional name of Hollinshead. In 1803 the estate passed to his nephew Lawrence Brock who also assumed the additional surname of Hollinshead. He sold the manor of Hollinshead to Eccles Shorrock, a Blackburn merchant and mill owner.

HOLLINSHEAD WELL

The Hall was abandoned and demolished when Liverpool Waterworks acquired the lands for water catchment.

Recently the site of the 18th-century hall and farm has been tidied up as part of a government aided scheme. The aim is to transform the site into an area for public recreation, incorporating the feature into the Roddleworth Nature Trail.

With the old well still, for the most part, in its original state and the ground plan of the buildings discernible by the low walls, the project should prove to be a most worthwhile venture.

Hollinshead Hall to Royal Arms

Leave by the old trackway and follow it up to go down to the left at top junction. This leads us down to cross the river bridge and pass through the kissing-gate on the right. Down the riverside path we wander to cross again by a flat bridge. Continue along the path to take another leading up to the right. Directly up we go till we reach the Royal Arms.

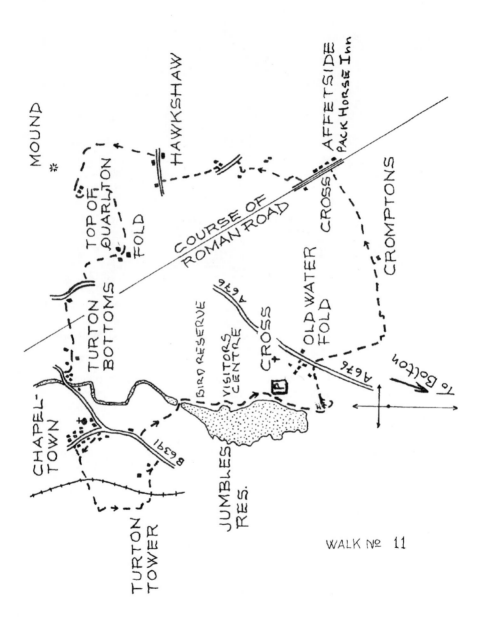

WALK No 11

Walk 11

A TRAMP
AROUND
TURTON

*Turton Tower, Affetside, Quarlton
and Chapeltown*

8 miles, 5 hours

MAP: *O.S. SD 61/71 PATHFINDER Series*

LUNCH: *Pack Horse, Affetside, or Chapeltown*

START: *Jumbles Information Centre*

Many visitors to the area visit Turton Tower, and maybe Chapletown or
Jumbles Nature Trail; few stray further. This walk is designed to explore a
few more of the area's ancient features. Jacobean farmsteads, ancient crosses,
a Roman road and a possible Bronze Age burial mound will be featured, all
set in an interesting landscape.

Jumbles Country Park

Jumbles Country Park lies in the Bradshaw Valley to the north of Bolton. It
was opened in 1971 following the construction of Jumbles Reservoir and
offers visitors a variety of activities including walking, fishing and picnicing
to choose from.

Jumbles Visitors Centre to Old Water Fold

*Follow the reservoir path to beyond the dam, down the steps and through the
small gateway. Follow the path around the quarry and up to where the stream
crosses the path. Turn left off the path and follow the small pathway above
the quarry to go over stile. Walk on to go over stile by tree. Follow right-hand
tree and hedge line to go through a gateway on the right before stile. Follow
tree-line up to go over a stile onto roadway. Water Fold is on your left.*

Old Water Fold

Old Water Fold is a substantial mullion fronted farmhouse overlooking Bradshaw Brook. The house bears a datestone of 1720 with the initials R B M (Bradshaw).

In the early 1900s the three Kershaw brothers lived here and ran it as a public house. The locals named the pub "The Three Bonny Lads" after the three big fellows who ran it. The brothers brewed and served their own ales and it was said to be so strong and thick that one could float a penny on top — sounds stronger than the ale that I myself brew!

Old Water Fold to Affetside

Walk up the lane opposite Old Water Fold to go over a stile in corner where the lane bends. Follow left-hand hedgerow/fence to go over a stile. Walk straight on to cross a brook and on to go over a stile onto lane and over a stile opposite.

Turn left and follow the iron fence round to follow left-hand wall onto a lane. Walk up the lane and straight on along the old track-way to go through a kissing-gate. Follow overhead lines to go through a gateway onto a path. Follow path to Affetside.

The Pack Horse Inn, Affetside

The Pack Horse was built in 1443 and some of the original timberwork and the ancient well from which water was drawn until recently — the Inn

had no mains water supply — remain intact. Above the fireplace in the old bar is the skull of George Whewell. It was Whewell who executed James the 7th Earl of Derby in 1651.

John Bridge often frequented the Inn until he was sentenced to death for counterfeiting in 1806. He was later reprieved and deported to Botany Bay, where his descendants today are amongst the wealthiest families in New South Wales.

The landlord is a very keen long distance walker, and you can always rely on a good welcome with an open fire and good food to set you up before the return leg.

Affetside Cross

Affetside Cross stands upon the old Roman road between Manchester and Ribchester. The cross is said to mark the half-way point between London and Edinburgh.

The Pack Horse Inn recalls a later use of the old Roman way. In centuries past, long lines of Galloway ponies would transport goods from the north-east Lancashire towns and villages to be traded in the great commercial centres of Manchester and Liverpool.

Affetside Cross, Roman Road.

Drovers' roads and track ways criss-cross the West Pennine Moors — a once vital network of communication and trade that today makes up the majority of footpaths used by walkers across the moors.

Affetside to Hawkshaw

On leaving the Pack Horse Inn turn right and walk along the road (the road follows the course of the Roman road here) past cottages to turn right after the last house. Follow left-hand wall to go over a stone stile. Follow left-hand wall, then fence, to go over fence stile. Cross field directly to go over next fence stile. Follow left-hand fence to go through a gate. Turn right and walk down the lane onto road.

Turn left and walk on to turn right by the first house, then left to walk between animal sheds onto field. Follow left-hand fence to go through a gate. Follow left-hand fence to go over fence (a stile missing). Follow left-hand fence down to go through a gap in fences to cross a brook. Walk past the sheds onto road. Turn right and walk into Hawkshaw.

Hawkshaw to Top of Quarlton

Follow path opposite the Red Lion pub to go through a stile by gateway. Follow path to go over stile by gate. Walk along the trackway to go through stile by gate. Follow left-hand wall up to go over a stile. Follow field boundary (the tumulus is over on your right) to go over a stile by a gate on the left to enter Top of Quarlton.

Carve Hill Tumulus

To the north east of Top of Quarlton stands Carve Hill upon the side of which stands a large steep-sided mound. The height of the mound on the west is 4.2 metres, and on the east 6.4 metres. Though there is no trace of a ditch, the mound is thought to have its origins in the Bronze Age and may be a large burial mound.

Quarlton

The hamlet of Quarlton is first mentioned in 1246 and the place-name is derived from the old German word 'quirn' meaning 'mill-stone'. The mining of mill-stones in the area is mentioned in 1332 and Quarlton probably formed the nucleus of the industry in the area at that time. The stone obtained from the moors above Edgworth is said to be one of the hardest grits in Britain, ideally suited for the manufacture of mill-stones.

During the 14th and 15th centuries the manor of Quarlton was held by the Knights Hospitalers, of whom the local families of Radcliffe and Barton held land. In 1570 Andrew Barton paid 16d. for the Lordship of Quarlton; he seems to have got a better deal than the later Levers of Hulme, soap barons, who craved such regal titles.

Top of Quarlton Farm has many styles of Jacobean Architecture — round-headed stone windows stand side by side with the more common straight-headed mullions, and peculiar doorheads abound. I would dearly love to investigate this structure more fully. On viewing it I am sure that you will agree with me that this is a most interesting and inviting dwelling.

Top of Quarlton to Quarlton Fold

Enter yard gate and walk past the front of the house, past the sheds into the field. Follow left-hand wall up to go over stile by gate onto trackway. Left, and walk down to the roadway. Right, to walk along the road to go over a stile in the fence on the right. Follow path through the wood to go over stile into field. Follow left-hand wall on down the field, veering right to go over stile in fence. Cross the field on a right diagonal to ruin. Walk down to enter Quarlton Fold.

Quarlton Fold

Quarlton Fold is a much altered 17th-century farmstead. A beam inside the barn is dated 1627 with the initials T.K.I.B.M. Above one of the barn door-ways is a dated door head of 1714 with the initials W.F.

Quarlton Fold to Chapeltown

Pass between side of farmhouse and barn to go through gate. Follow track-way on to field gate. Walk down the field to go through a gate onto road. Turn right and walk along the road to go left down the driveway at the footpath sign after the first house. Walk down the drive and over the stile to follow right-hand wall, then fence to go over a stile and down the steps. Turn right then left and walk past the old factory to follow cobbled lane onto road. Turn left and walk on to turn right at junction. Walk up High Street to Chapeltown.

Chapeltown

Chapeltown is an attractive moorland village of 17th- and 18th-century stone cottages. The main axis of the village is High Street with the Chetham Arms — an 18th-century inn — and the old stocks and cross at its northern end.

The market cross marked the centre of Turton Fair, a well known and popular livestock fair held in the village until early this century. In 1885 the stocks and cross were moved to the grounds of Turton Tower. They were then renovated and brought back in the 1930s to stand in the Village Garden which was donated to the village by Miss Annie Barlow.

Chapeltown to Turton Tower

From the corner of the Chetham Arms walk down Kay Street and on along the cobbled lane to cross the railway. Go through kissing-gate at the corner of the house opposite. Follow left-hand wall up onto a lane. Turn left and walk along the lane to go through a kissing-gate. Take the lane on the left and walk down to go over a bridge to enter Turton Tower.

Turton Tower

The manor of Turton was a part of the barony of Manchester, assessed as one plough land in the earliest record. It was held chiefly by Richard de Lathom in 1212 as part of a knights fee. In 1302, it descended to the de Tarbocks, who were actually junior members of the Lathom family.

With the death of John de Tarbock in 1420 the house and estate were left to his daughter Elizabeth, Tarbock in Merseyside being secured by the male heir.

Elizabeth married William Orrell of Wigan and Turton became the seat of the Orrells. In 1596 a later William Orrell built the tower that we can, for the most part, still see today. By 1628 the Orrell family was in serious debt to a Manchester money lender and textile merchant, Humphrey Chetham, who acquired the house. Chetham did not need Turton as a home and let the Orrells remain in residence until 1648.

It remained in Chetham hands until it was sold to James Kay in 1835. The Kays restored the tower in grand Victorian style and enjoyed a lifestyle to match. In 1890 it was sold again, and again in 1903. Its last owner, Lady Nina Knowles, presented the tower to the Turton Urban District Council in 1930 and it became the Council Chamber.

With local government re-organisation in 1974 Turton became part of the new borough of Blackburn and the tower is now a museum. The majority of the tower's contents came from the demolished Bradshaw Hall which stood nearby, bequeathed by the late Colonel Hardcastle.

The tower is an L-shaped building, originating in a pele tower, probably of the 15th century, with the remains of a spiral staircase in the north-east corner and an Elizabethan top storey. In 1596 the detached farmhouse was remodelled and attached to the pele, this work is partly timber-framed, partly of stone. The later ornate timbering is part of the work undertaken by Joseph Kay from 1835.

Turton Tower to Jumbles Visitors Centre

Walk down the lane onto the road. Turn left & walk on to go over stile by a gate on right. Walk straight up to follow right-hand fence to pass over stile. Follow the path to go over a bridge. Turn right & walk along the path by the reservoir, passing the Bird Reserve to the Visitors Centre and Car Park.

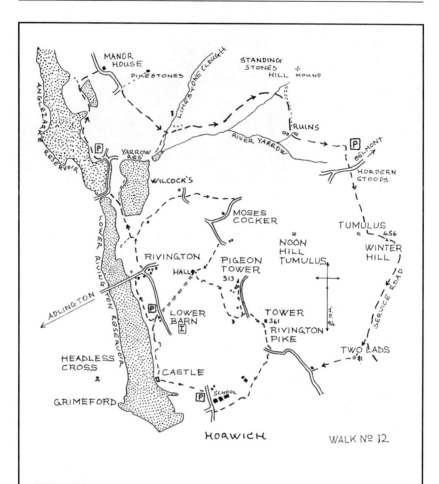

WALK Nº 12

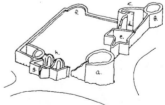

**PLAN OF THE LIVERPOOL
CASTLE REPLICA**
a) Great Tower
b) Castle Keep
c) Chapel
d) Great Hall
e) Kitchens
f) South-east Tower
g) Barbican & Outer Gate
h) Gatehouse

SEE PAGE 129

GREAT BARN HOUSE

Walk 12

CRUCKS
AND
CASTLES

Rivington Country Park & Winter Hill

11 miles, 6 hours or

6 & 4¹/₂ miles shorter walks

MAP:	*O.S. SD 61/71 PATHFINDER Series*
LUNCH:	*Lower Barn or packed lunch*
START:	*Lower Barn Information Centre*

The best starting point for all three walks is Rivington Lower Barn, having a good car park, toilets and refreshments.

The longer walk leaves the Lower Barn to visit Rivington Village, the Yarrow Valley, Winter Hill, Rivington Pike and Liverpool Castle. The shorter walks take in some of the old farms, Rivington Hall Barn, the Tower & Pike and the Castle. Easy walking with lots to explore, the choice is yours.

Rivington Lower Barn

Great House Barn, referred to as Lower Barn, is constructed of large oak crucks, each side being taken from the same tree. This type of building frame has been used from the earliest times up until the late 17th century when the number of great oaks had declined almost to extinction. So widely had the great forests become depleted during this period that Charles I led a campaign to start a programme of re-forestation throughout the kingdom.

Lower Barn was built in the 16th century and has been added to and rebuilt several times over the years. Today it houses an Information Centre for visitors to the West Pennine Moors and a small cafe. The adjacent stone building with mullioned windows was once Great House Farm. This has now been converted to provide a craft shop, rangers' office and public toilets.

The Rivington Lower Barn Head

This damaged stone head can be found on display inside Rivington Lower Barn. It was found by workmen during the excavations for the Yarrow Reservoir. Although referred to as a 'Celtic' head, its true origins are obscure. But given such ancient

THE YARROW HEAD

settlement in the area a pre-Conquest origin is more than probable.

Lower Barn to Rivington Village (Longer Walk)

On leaving the Lower Barn walk down past the picnic area and take the woodland path above the reservoir that leads to the roadway at Rivington School. Right, then left at fork to walk down to the village green and church.

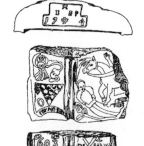

Rivington Church and School

The first building of architectural interest one notices on approaching Rivington from the west is the school. It was rebuilt in 1714, on the site of the ancient free grammar school founded by Bishop Pilkington in 1566.

The church was first built around 1540, but only a few windows and the pulpit remain from that period.

For the most part the church represents the rebuilding of around 1666. Inside is a monument to John Shawe, who died in 1627, in the form of a large brass plate with a skeleton on a mattress at the bottom.

Rivington Unitarian Chapel

The Unitarian chapel was founded in 1662 and built in 1703, being one of the oldest of its kind in the country.

It is built on a plain oblong plan with cross windows. The inside is furnished with box pews and the pulpit is in the middle of the north side.

In the churchyard, by the gate, can be found a collection of decorated lintels from earlier houses of the district. The dates on the stones range from 1695 to 1732.

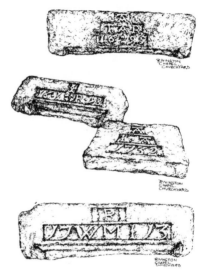

Rivington Village to Manor House

Pass through the kissing-gate at the bottom of the village green. The path leads us via stiles to meet with a wide trackway. Walk up to the left then pass by the gate on the right. This track leads us along by Yarrow Reservoir to go left at fork, down through the woods to the road. Right, and walk on to go left at road junction and on to enter Anglezarke Car Park & Picnic Area.

Pass through gate and walk on above the reservoir and on up and along by the higher reservoir. Walk down below the dam head and up a path at the other side that leads us up through the woods to Manor House.

Manor House & Pikestones

See Walk 7 for details.

Manor House to Winter Hill

Walk up the road to leave by access trackway on left that leads down to the
bottom of Limestone Clough. Follow the rough road up to the left to pass
over stile by gate. Continue along the track, over stile by gate and on a fair
way to go right at junction, over and down to the stream by the ruins of
Lower & Higher Hempshaw's.

Leave the main path and take the boundary path that leads up to the left to
meet with a wall. Follow wall down to the road at Hordern Stoops and pass
over stile opposite. The path leads us up to the summit of Winter Hill.

Rivington Moor Bronze Age Sites

Many Bronze Age sites are to be found on the moors around Winter Hill, and
on the edge of the Rivington Moor plateau three substantial sites can easily be
made out.

To the south stands a cairn complex known as 'Two Lads'. On the west can
be seen the Noon Hill tumulus, a disturbed round cairn with traces of a
central burial. Some years ago an excavation found several secondary crema-

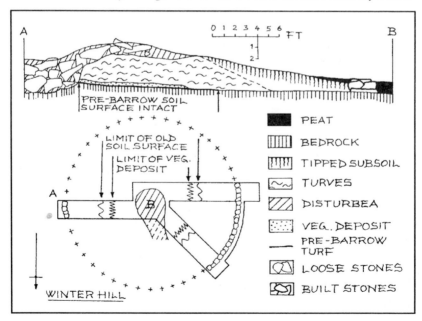

tions, one being in an enlarged food vessel in a small stone cist. The latter, plus some barbed and tanged arrowheads found during the excavation, is on display in Bolton Museum. The third site is the composite cairn which stands near the summit of Winter Hill.

The Winter Hill tumulus was excavated in 1958 to determine the nature of its structure (the primary burial chamber had been robbed during an earlier excavation by 'treasure hunters') which was seen to be remarkably well-preserved.

The diagram shows a plan of the cairn and a section at A-B. A kerb, 2 feet wide and approximately 18 inches high surrounded the mound. Inside this was a rising layer of subsoil, on the outer edges a large turf layer. These large sods, which formed the inner part of the mound, were up to 3 feet across and in one case 9 inches thick and for the most part placed upside-down.

Below this was a fibrous and matted layer of well-preserved vegetable matter, quite free from soil. In this compressed matter, remains of whinberry, ferns, cotton-grass, heather, mosses and birch-twigs, as well as an axe-cut piece of birch pole 3 inches in diameter and 20 inches long, were identifiable. The centre of the mound was seen to be a much disturbed cairn of stones.

The picture shows a possible reconstruction of what this type of structure would have looked like in its heyday: a turf-roofed round-house with a central stone hearth — smoke would escape through the turf cap-vent. The turfs would have been laid upside down, except for the top-

BRONZE AGE HUT
(RING CAIRN) TURTON

most layer, to form an in-grown thatch effect. The vegetation layer represents the debris left behind when the hut was abandoned. The site can be placed in the local Early Bronze Age before the period of valley settlement.

For a better understanding of Bronze Age people the archaeologist would do well to study the living patterns and settlement of the North American Indians during the 17th and 18th century. For the general reader, may I suggest Colin Renfrew's *"Before Civilization"* as being the best guide to the prehistoric periods in Europe.

Winter Hill Masts to the Two Lads

Walk along the service road down to where a path leads up to the three stone cairns, two of which are known as the Two Lads.

The Two Lads to Rivington Pike

Walk down towards the reservoir to pick up a good path that leads down to the road at Pike Cottage. Walk past the cottage and up the road to leave by a track on the right that leads up to the Pike.

Rivington Pike Tower

The Pike Tower was built in 1733 by John Andrews to demonstrate, it is said, his ownership of the surrounding land. The tower was built on the site of an ancient fire beacon.

In an age before rapid communications, the lighting of a fire beacon on a prominent hill was a quick way of spreading news of national emergencies. Records show that the Pike beacon was lit on the night of July 19th to warn that the Spanish Armada had entered the English Channel.

In recent years the Pike beacon has been lit to mark national celebrations: Queen Elizabeth's Silver Jubilee in 1977 and the Royal Wedding in 1981 being such occasions.

A fair has been held at the Pike for many years. Before 1900 it was held on Whit Sunday, but in 1900 it was changed to Good Friday. Since 1932 this has become an annual event attracting large numbers of visitors. The Good Friday Fair is followed on Easter Saturday by the Pike Race which attracts around 300 runners.

On a clear day excellent panoramic views of the surrounding area can be enjoyed from Rivington Pike. The Welsh mountains, the Isle of Man and the Cumbrian fells all come into view. The Bronze Age sites on Noon Hill, Winter Hill and Two Lads Hummock can also be made out from this point.

Rivington Pike to Liverpool Castle

Return to the road and pass through stile by gate opposite. Follow the path down, through gates and down the lane, past the school to the road. Right, and walk along the road then cross to enter wood at bridleway. This track leads down to the Castle.

The Liverpool Castle Folly

On a small rise on the eastern shore of Lower Rivington Reservoir, known as Coblowe, stands a replica of the ruined Liverpool Castle. This was built by the soap manufacturer and industrialist W. H. Lever after he purchased the Rivington Hall estate in 1900 and turned much of it into Lever Park.

The re-creation of the ruin was started in 1912 using locally quarried stone, but finances were short and progress was slow and when Lever died in 1925 work on the project ceased altogether.

The original Liverpool Castle was built around 1235 by William de Ferrers, Earl of Derby. Between 1660 and 1685 the garrison was removed and the castle partly dismantled. The castle was finally demolished in 1725.

Liverpool Castle to Lower Barn

A path leads above the reservoir to the Lower Barn Information Centre.

THE SHORTER WALKS

No 1:
6 miles. (Rivington Village to Rivington Pike section)

Pass through kissing gate at the bottom of the village green. The path leads us via stiles to meet with a wide trackway. Right, and walk on to go over stile on right. Follow right-hand fence to go over stile and on to pass through kising gate on to road. Walk up to the left to Wilcock's Farm.

Wilcock's Farm

Wilcock's is a much altered and modernised 17th-century farmhouse. The ground floor is fairly intact to the left of the main doorway. The first floor level has been raised to hold a new slated roof. Above the doorway is a dated doorhead of 1670 with the initials R.I.E.

Wilcock's Farm to Moses Cocker's

Go over a stile by a gate on the side of the barn to go over next stile. Follow old trackway to go over a stile and on, to go over another stile. Follow left-hand fence, then wall, to turn right by a gate on the left. Follow track to go through a gate on to road. Turn right and walk on. Moses Cocker's is the first house on the right.

Moses Cocker's

Moses Cocker's is another attractive 17th-century farmhouse, the doorhead of which is dated 1693 with the initials C. R.R.A.M.

Moses Cocker's to Rivington Hall Barn

Walk on along the road to T-junction. Turn left and walk on to turn right at the next lane. Follow lane to enter Rivington Hall Barn through a gate.

Rivington Hall Barn

This barn adjoins Rivington Hall, and is linked to Lower Barn by Hall Drive, a walk of about 5 minutes. The barn was originally used for agricultural purposes. During the winter months, livestock from nearby farms, together with their feed, were sheltered here. Later the barn was used solely as a hay store. Today the barn is used to host social functions and is a well known and loved landmark to the people of the surrounding district.

Rivington Hall

In the 17th century, Rivington Hall was the home of the Breres family. The initials of William Breres and his wife Martha appear on three of the building's datestones — 1694, 1700 and 1713. The hall was sold to John Andrews of Bolton in 1729, and his descendant, Robert Andrews, rebuilt the front of the hall in 1774.

HALL
BARN

Rivington Hall Barn to Pigeon Tower

Walk up the lane on the left in front of the hall to turn left at fork. Walk on to go through a kissing gate and on up the terraced path to Pigeon Tower.

PIGEON
TOWER

Lord Leverhulme's Moorland Garden

The hillside gardens were laid out in 1905 by T. H. Mawson for Lord Leverhulme, a fervent advocate of landscape architecture.

Upon this bleak hillside were built drives, terraces, lawns and water gardens. It is all now overgrown and in a state of natural decay.

The bungalow, rebuilt after being burnt by suffragettes, has, like the lodges, been demolished by the Liverpool Corporation, but numerous garden buildings remain, the most prominent being the Dovecote Tower, contributing to a picturesque skyline.

The ruins of several sets of loggias and terraces, and a bridge carrying a path over one of the drives, can also be made out.

To the north east of the Dovecote Tower lie the Bronze Age sites of Noon Hill and Winter Hill, and further north across the Yarrow Valley lies the kerbed mound of Standing Stone Hill.

Standing Stones Hill

Below Round Loaf, to the south east, at a height of 1,000 feet O.D., lies Standing Stones Hill. On its southerly edge can be found a kerbed mound with a stone retaining circle. It is this stone circle which gives the hill its name. The site appears to be intact and no archaeological investigations are recorded apart from the site location.

Pigeon Tower to Rivington Pike

Follow the road to turn left on the path leading up to the tower.

THE SHORTER WALKS

No 2:

4½ miles (Rivington Barns, Tower, Pike & Castle)

Walk up the drive from the Lower Barn to Rivington Hall Barn and then follow previous directions.

After finishing your walk you may wish to visit the tiny village of Grimeford to see the Headless Cross.

The Headless Cross, Grimeford

The Headless Cross at Anderton can be found by the roadside at a cross roads on a minor road behind the Millstone Hotel on the A673. The cross and stocks are said to stand at the centre of the ancient village of Grimeford.

The cross shaft is of an early, possibly 11th or 10th century, date. The legs

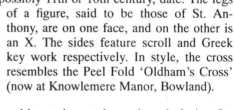

HEADLESS CROSS
GRIMEFORD

of a figure, said to be those of St. Anthony, are on one face, and on the other is an X. The sides feature scroll and Greek key work respectively. In style, the cross resembles the Peel Fold 'Oldham's Cross' (now at Knowlemere Manor, Bowland).

Mounted upon the ancient shafts is a flat sign-post stone pointing the way to Blegburn, Bolton, Wigan and Preston — the spelling for Blackburn is how it used to be pronounced in my youth.